LIVING
IN THE
Present
MOMENT

a Divine Design

Dearest Tova,
So good to see you! Celebrate all your moments in time!
Love,
Teena

ELLYN HUTT
&
TEENA SLATKIN

3/1/02
Dear Tova,
Cherish each and every moment!
love you,
Ellyn

AvivA
BOOKS
Denver, Colorado

Living in the Present Moment: A Divine Design
Published by AivA Books
Denver, CO

Names: Hutt, Ellyn, author. Slatkin, Teena, author.
Title: Living in the present moment : a divine design / Ellyn Hutt and Teena Slatkin.
Description: Denver [Colorado] : AivA Books, 2019. | Also available as an ebook.
Identifiers: ISBN: 978-0-578-48381-8
Subjects: LCSH: Happiness. | Self-help techniques. | Spiritual healing. | Spirituality—Judaism.
BISAC: SELF-HELP / Personal Growth / Happiness
Classification: LCC BM729.S44 | DDC 296.76–dc22

Cover and Interior Design by Victoria Wolf
Editing by Vicki Tosher

QUANTITY PURCHASES: Schools, companies, professional groups, clubs, and other organizations may qualify for special terms when ordering quantities of this title. For information, email livinginthepresent.book@gmail.com.

To our loving parents who gave us wisdom,

Our precious children who inspire us
and give us hope for the future,

Our cherished grandchildren who fill us
with wonder as they grow,

And our husbands, our soul mates, who
love us with complete devotion.

TABLE OF CONTENTS

PREFACE

THIS BOOK HAS BEEN TESTED, not in a laboratory, but in real life and on real people. Throughout the past twenty years that we've been working on this book, we have experienced the lessons about living in the present moment that we are sharing with you. We could write another book just about how we used the insights, wisdom, and images presented within each chapter to guide us through life's challenges, opportunities, and celebrations.

Between the two of us, we've sent children off to college and on to their own careers, married off children, and gained daughters-in-law and sons-in-law. We have both lost parents to prolonged illness and to sudden death. We've changed jobs, survived, and healed from major surgeries, become grandmothers, faced financial challenges, celebrated joyful holidays, and marked milestone birthdays, all while living our everyday lives.

Through it all, we have turned time and again to the wisdom we are focused on sharing with you here. We didn't anticipate that each chapter was going to come to life for us, jumping off the pages and into our hearts, minds, and souls giving us personal inspiration and direction. We didn't know that would happen, but what it tells you is that these ideas are not merely theoretical or hypothetical or philosophical. We know they work because we have put them into practice and have experienced success.

We began this project to invite Jewish people, who frequently seek spirituality, to investigate the wisdom of their own enduring, centuries-old heritage. There are a plethora of books with New Age to Buddhist perspectives that address living in the present moment, some even authored by Jewish writers. However, what we did not find was a book that directly addresses living in the present moment, based on Jewish tradition, that is presented in an accessible way. What we are presenting is more than a Jewish flavor of the same idea. There are fundamental differences between other philosophies and Judaism that Jewish people deserve to know and understand.

It gives us great joy to share ancient wisdom that has not only withstood the test of time but wisdom we also put into practice in our lives regularly. We hope you will find the insights and direction provided by *Living in the Present Moment: A Divine Design* as valuable as we have.

Ellyn and Teena

ACKNOWLEDGMENTS

WE ARE DEEPLY GRATEFUL for the opportunity we have had to create this book and for the many people who have helped us bring this book to you, our readers. We express our thanks to the following people:

Our family and friends, who maintained interest in our project. Their ongoing excitement and enthusiasm kept us motivated and moving forward.

Our students and colleagues, who have patiently waited for this book to arrive and who inspired and encouraged us to continue writing over the span of the many years it took to create it.

Sharlene Ancell Kark, Ellyn's mom of blessed memory, who read the text and offered suggestions to strengthen the clarity and accessibility of our writing and gave us confidence in our ability to make the project a reality.

Aileen Leben, Teena's mom of blessed memory, who had

such pride in our work and inspired us with her joyful anticipation of the book's completion.

Lecia Sud, Teena's sister, who gave us helpful, necessary input and suggestions.

Sue Shefman, Teena's sister who read the book and offered heart-felt suggestions and encouragement.

Susan Berson, a friend who devoted time to help us perfect our manuscript and gave us her professional guidance and input.

Andrea Hyatt, a friend, who read our manuscript and offered helpful suggestions.

Buddy Slatkin, Teena's husband, who handled the legal work involved in producing this book, read the manuscript, and encouraged our vision and efforts.

Steve Hutt, Ellyn's husband, who spent many hours diligently editing our final draft with skill and expertise when we could no longer see what needed to be changed. He supported our vision and encouraged our efforts.

Polly Letofsky, owner of My Word Publishing, whose professional expertise, guidance, and confidence in our project, helped us to manage and complete all of the detailed steps of the publishing process. She guided us to all of the right people for us to work with along the way.

Vicki Tosher, our editor and supporter, who became our friend through many conversations during the editing process. She went above and beyond in reviewing our manuscript and offering detailed suggestions and corrections to improve the quality of our work.

Sue Miller, of blessed memory, who shortly before her passing happened to mention to Teena that she thought that Vicki Tosher and Polly Letofsky would be the ideal people for us to work with. We are forever grateful for her intuitive insight and suggestion.

Victoria Wolf, who created our cover design and interior layout and patiently listened to our ideas and captured our vision with a design that perfectly conveys our message.

Bobby Haas, a writer with My Word Publishing, who helped us refine and redirect the Introduction to our book, streamlining our ideas and focusing on the main points we wanted to write about.

David Sanders, Sari Horovitz, and Risa Aqua -- Ellyn's initial writing group that provided the foundation for what our book evolved into being.

Evelyn Hutt, Ellyn's sister-in-law, for her encouragement and help to stay on track with our writing.

Zahava Koll, a friend and colleague, who was the first to say, "You should write a book," and who throughout the years maintained enthusiasm about the potential benefit our book would have to inspire Jewish women.

Rabbi Bar Ami of Rehovot, Israel, for his encouragement and conviction that the Jewish world was truly waiting for our book to come into being.

Rabbi Hillel Goldberg, Publisher of the *Intermountain Jewish News* and published author of Jewish works, who encouraged us to bring this book to fruition.

Creator of the Universe, to God, who gave each of us everything and everyone we needed to make this book happen. We are grateful for our good health, endurance, resources, vision, inspiration, guidance, and direction.

We are also grateful for each other, and for the partnership and deep friendship that we have developed and shared for more than a decade. We enjoyed each and every session we spent working together while creating this book.

Our final acknowledgment is to you, our readers. While we were writing this book, you were a significant part of our journey. We always had you in mind.

INTRODUCTION:

A NEW PERSPECTIVE ON THE PRESENT MOMENT

WOULDN'T IT BE ENCHANTING if you woke up each morning filled with a sense of peaceful awareness and joyful enthusiasm for your life right now? Wouldn't it be refreshing if you could hold onto this sense of centeredness and well-being throughout each day and throughout your life, regardless of the circumstances you were facing? And wouldn't it be exciting to discover that you already have everything you need to reach and maintain this state of healthy living? The answer to these questions is, of course: "Yes, yes, and yes."

Many would answer, and perhaps you have heard, that the key to achieving these goals is to "live in the present moment." That sounds good, but how do we do it? Many New Age thinkers and writers advise and suggest that we can achieve that goal only by letting go of the past and not thinking about the future—just living for today. What is the basis of that advice? It is based on the belief that remembering the past often takes people to places of pain and regret, which is immobilizing, and that thinking about the future is likely to cause worries and fears, which is also immobilizing. Hence the logic, and the advice, that it's best not to think about the past or the future—just live for today.

However, this perspective and the advice derived from it are illogical. Let's think for a moment. We normally *mourn* the loss of memory—whether through amnesia, dementia, or some other mental challenge. So, why would anyone suggest that trying to forget their past could be a good thing? Our pasts have much to teach us. The same can be said about imagination and thinking about the future. Someone who isn't able to think about the future cannot plan, anticipate consequences, dream, or prepare. Would we seriously think that imposing this handicap on ourselves could somehow help us live more rewarding lives? In addition to the irrationality of this argument is the fact that healthy, normal human beings aren't really capable of turning off their memory or stifling their imagination.

MEMORY AND IMAGINATION ARE ESSENTIAL

Memory and imagination are vital parts of what make us the amazing human beings that we are. Memory and imagination are tremendous gifts from God, our Creator, given specifically to help us fulfill our potential in this world. These gifts are also critical and essential components of fully living in the present moment. Memories of the past are there to ground us with wisdom; visualizing the future is there to guide us with inspiration.

Since people are meant to flourish using their memory and imagination, how is it then that people end up using these special gifts in ways that prevent them from fulfilling their potential? What goes wrong? The answer is that it's the *misuse* of memory and imagination that causes people to be immobilized by pain, regret, worry, and fear.

WE HAVE A CHOICE

The challenge is that we have a choice in how we use these powerful gifts. Memory and imagination can be misused easily and misdirected. Unless these gifts are directed actively and intentionally in a positive way, their natural course will likely be toward the negative, bringing a person to a state of unhappiness.

When memory holds us captive to what happened in the past, we cannot respond to what is actually going on, right now in the present. Misusing memory to relive pain, and to be paralyzed with guilt while experiencing past mistakes as if they were happening right now, blocks all of the light from our lives. When all of the light is blocked, we cannot, and do not, see the next step that is possible. We remain stuck in mental and emotional obstacles, and get caught endlessly reacting to and reenacting our past thoughts and actions. Misusing memory causes us to live in fear; this fear distorts our perception of the present and projects negativity onto and into the future. We remain stuck and we suffer.

When we are stuck living in the past, the future also feels stunted and limited. This perspective leads us to misuse our imagination, and we cannot see that the future can be different than the past has been. We have no hope because we cannot imagine how things could get better. We misuse the gift of imagination to conjure up visions of a future that are frightening and overwhelming, causing us to avoid taking any action at all. The pain continues. To a person who misuses imagination, even good memories of past successes are discounted—they appear to be flukes that do not inspire confidence or hope; to the contrary, the memories increase thoughts and feelings of anxiety and insecurity. Those sad outcomes have prompted the misplaced advice described above to forego one's memory and imagination in the hope that by blocking them out, the present moment can be enjoyed.

Quite the opposite is true. Memory, when used correctly, is for gleaning wisdom, building our foundation for growth, and increasing our sensitivity and compassion. Imagination is meant to be used to create and connect to an inspiring vision of the future that illuminates our path and directs our decisions in the here and now. The choice we need to make is *how* we are going to look at what we remember from the past and *what* we are going to visualize about the future. Once we identify healthy ways to use our memory and imagination, we can, with practice, develop the skills we need to use these gifts properly. Within the pages of this book, you will discover how to apply these skills in positive and productive ways. You will learn how to use your memory to extract wisdom and life lessons from painful past challenges, and you will learn how to use your imagination to focus on inspiring visions of the future.

There is another interesting dynamic that is also involved with these forces. We are where our thoughts are; we live in the framework that our thoughts create. Thoughts influence and shape our speech and our actions. However, the reverse is also true. Our speech and actions also have the ability to affect our thoughts. How we direct our thoughts about the past and the future, how we use our words, and how we act in each situation, all converge and interrelate determining whether we move in a positive or a negative direction. Therefore, working on our thoughts, words, and actions has a profound impact on bringing us into the present moment, where we can achieve a place of dynamic centeredness and fulfillment. This might sound overwhelming. Where do we start? This book will lead you on a step-by-step discovery of how to make this a creative and joyful process.

ANCIENT WISDOM FOR TODAY'S WORLD

What is fascinating and profoundly meaningful to discover and know is that the ancient and eternal teachings of Torah, woven into Jewish life and traditions, provide a design for this very process. Although for many people the definition of "Torah" is the first five books of the Bible (Genesis, Exodus, Leviticus, Numbers, and Deuteronomy), we will be looking at Torah in an all-encompassing way. Torah means instruction and includes all the wisdom of our tradition, whether found in an exploratory explanation of a Torah personality, a beloved and established holiday custom or ritual, the nuance of a Hebrew word, or a detail of Jewish law.

We call all of this Torah and, taken together, it provides us with the guidelines we can use to live our lives in the present moment. Torah instructs us with spiritual, yet practical, ways to use the gifts of memory and imagination, along with our thoughts, words, and actions to help us thrive. We want to bring this wisdom alive for you in a new and accessible way.

A DIVINE DESIGN FOR LIVING IN THE PRESENT MOMENT

In *Living in the Present Moment*, we call this comprehensive and multidimensional package of Torah wisdom a Divine Design. Think of the Divine Design as a blueprint for living. If you were building a physical house, you would strive to design one that is solid, healthy, and joyful to live in. Similarly, you should also want to design a life structure of thoughts, words, and actions that is solid, healthy, and joyful to live within. Following this Divine Design will guide you to use your thoughts, words, and actions to create a beautiful environment in which you can live and flourish.

We call the ideal structure which emerges from implementing the Divine Design in your life the "House of the Present Moment." We use the metaphor of a house to represent this structure because the parallels to a physical home are compelling. In order to be safe and comfortable, our physical house needs to be well-designed and carefully built with close attention paid to detail. It also needs to be maintained on a regular basis. *Your* House of the Present Moment requires the same approach. Every one of your thoughts, words, and actions, like the details of a blueprint, impacts the quality of the structure you are building, determining how you experience life and how you respond to your circumstances.

The metaphor of a house helps us appreciate that this building process is multidimensional and that there are different facets that we need to address. In a physical house, we have different rooms that serve different purposes. Our House of the Present Moment has "rooms" as well, representing the wisdom implanted and revealed in specific aspects of Jewish life and living. Each room in the House of the Present Moment explores distinct opportunities we have been given to practice living in the present moment. And it does take practice. We can't just suddenly decide, "I'm going to live in the present moment." We need certain skills that have to be understood and activated in different ways and in different circumstances on an ongoing basis.

LEARNING AND LIVING A PRESENT-MOMENT LIFE

Fortunately, these skills can be learned, and the way to learn them is right at your fingertips. The rooms of the home we are about to show you will be rooms where you can learn how to use the strength of your *memory* to extract wisdom from the past rather than dragging around increasingly heavier loads of pain. The rooms will also let you learn how you can use the power of your *imagination* to create an inspiring vision, rather than to conjure up frightening images that immobilize you. You will be able to learn how to practice and strengthen your ability to live in the present moment with your thoughts, words, and actions.

The beauty of using the Divine Design as your blueprint is

that it enables you to work on building your House of the Present Moment from multiple angles. As you continue to build, you will experience a shift in your perspective and your emotions. You will begin to see ripple effects. You will notice that implementing the Divine Design is a dynamic process that impacts every aspect of your life.

The Divine Design has the power to be transformative and, at the same time, be grounded and down-to-earth. As we take you on a tour of the House of the Present Moment and into each of its special rooms, you will find out what these life skills are and how to practice them. Exploring the different rooms, complete with cozy alcoves that highlight particular features of the Divine Design, will show you how to use various insights to build and live in your own House of the Present Moment.

After you become familiar with the book, you can revisit any room in the House of the Present Moment at any time to remind yourself how you truly want to live. If you find yourself facing a particular challenge or slipping into misusing memory or imagination, you can fix it. If you realize that you have mistakenly left the House of the Present Moment and have entered the House of the Painful Past or the House of the Frightening Future, you don't have to stay there. You don't need to remain in the dysfunctional duplex of pain and fear that those kinds of houses represent. You can quickly re-center yourself by simply going back to the House of the Present Moment and reconnecting to the Divine Design of the room and the inspiration that you most need to guide you. The table of contents tells you which specific ideas or skills each room addresses.

The Divine Design is a gift we have been given to help us live our lives to the fullest. It is the necessary companion to the gifts of memory and imagination that each of us has been given to help us reach our potential. When you use the Divine Design to build your House of the Present Moment, you will discover that you can indeed awaken each morning filled with a sense of peaceful awareness and joyful enthusiasm for your life right now. You will discover that you can stay centered and experience a state of well-being throughout every day. Regardless of the circumstances you are facing, you will discover that you can flourish. Your House of the Present Moment will be a beautiful and inspiring place in which to live and grow. Everything you need to know, in order to build and actively maintain this vibrant house, is ready for you to explore and learn in the pages that follow. Let's begin.

ENTERING THE HOUSE

As we make our way toward the House of the Present Moment,
we notice that there is a sense of tranquility and peace
surrounding this house that draws us closer.
Heading up the walkway, bordered by colorful flowers,
we are greeted by an expansive, elegant home.
The front of the house is graced with tall arched windows that
embrace the light of the outdoors and flood the rooms
from floor to ceiling.
The doorway beckons us in
with a sign that practically sings ...

"WELCOME TO THE HOUSE OF THE PRESENT MOMENT"

I.

Miriam's Courtyard

INTRODUCTION

AS WE ENTER the House of the Present Moment, we find ourselves in the foyer. Framed by a welcoming archway, we catch sight of a ray of light casting its soft glow into the area where we are standing. As we walk towards the light and peek through the archway to see where it is coming from, we realize that we also hear the faint sound of water—at first it is only the splashing of a softly bubbling fountain, but as we draw closer, we also hear the steady rippling of a gently flowing stream. The mixture of sounds creates a melody that lures us further in until we see that although we have come into the house, we are again outside, finding ourselves in a large courtyard. With shade trees, lush bushes, and vibrant flowers bordering the small stream from which we heard the soft sounds before, now the sweet fragrance of this garden surrounds us.

BEGINNING OUR JOURNEY INTO THE COURTYARD ...

Let's take a moment to feel the calm, yet invigorating, tranquility that envelops us as we stroll together through this courtyard. Here, it is the physical environment—the natural beauty and fragrance of the trees and flowers, the soothing sound of the water, and the secure feeling of a cozy courtyard—that creates our deep sense of serenity. A feeling of peaceful centeredness is not dependent on our circumstances or surroundings; once we experience that feeling, we can evoke it as a state of being to carry with us regardless of where we are. This is the feeling that comes from living life more fully in the present moment. It is the feeling of being in the flow, keenly aware of what is happening and, at the same time, being relaxed as we navigate through our lives.

A courtyard with a fountain, wooden benches surrounding it, a flowing stream, and beautiful flowers and shade trees would be comforting enough by itself. However, this courtyard is unique. This courtyard is called Miriam's Courtyard, and the design of everything relates to her essence and special ability to live in the present moment.

WHO IS MIRIAM,
AND WHY IS THIS MIRIAM'S COURTYARD?

The prophet Micah said in God's name: "When I brought you up from the Land of Egypt and redeemed you from the house of slavery, I sent before you Moses, Aaron, and Miriam." (Micah 6:4). Moses was our teacher, Aaron our high priest, and Miriam helped to build the nation they led. As we'll come to see, Miriam, who was the sister of Moses and Aaron and a prophetess in her own right, lived her life completely in the present moment and nurtured others to do the same. This courtyard lets us physically experience how the internal state of being in the present moment feels, giving us a hint of the tranquility that comes from developing and nurturing a life lived in the present moment.

Just as a child or an adult who might go out to her great-grandmother's old apple tree in the middle of the family's yard to feel her great-grandmother's presence, reconnect to her dreams, and bask in the memories that provide inspiration, we come to Miriam's Courtyard. Here, we can feel her presence and remind ourselves of all that she did to show us the way of living in the present and her legacy of inspiration. As we explore this courtyard, we'll come to know more about Miriam and why her courtyard sits in the heart of the House of the Present Moment.

As we look around the courtyard more closely, we see more delicately arched doorways that beckon us into other rooms of the house, designed so that no matter where we are, we are never more than a few steps away from these beautiful surroundings. As our eyes adjust to the bright light, we spot wooden benches tucked under the spreading branches of shade trees inviting us to come, sit, and enjoy the peace of the courtyard. When we look around, we count four benches, one on each side of the courtyard. Engraved into the wood of each bench are verses from the Torah and our *midrashim* (our oral tradition) that tell us about Miriam's life. We'll come back to read each one and learn more about her life—the wisdom that guided her, the vision that inspired her, and the choices she made in each moment to elevate herself and all of those around her.

MIRIAM'S FOUNTAIN— WHY WAS WATER, A FUNDAMENTAL SOURCE OF LIFE, CONNECTED TO MIRIAM'S ESSENCE?

Strolling around, we notice that the fountain is always within our sight. A water fountain in a courtyard isn't such an unusual thing, but this one is special. Here in Miriam's Courtyard, it sits in the very center because its flowing water symbolizes the essence of Miriam's life and spiritual message, and it gives us the imagery and language to understand her.

The fountain, a continuous flow of water, is reminiscent of the well of water that our tradition teaches us that God provided for the Jewish people in Miriam's merit for forty years while they wandered in the desert. Miriam's life was deeply connected to water, both physically and as a metaphor for living in flow of the present moment. For this reason, Miriam's righteousness merited water to be provided for all the Jewish people she inspired and taught.

LET'S BEGIN HERE AND WE'LL DISCOVER MORE ...

Spiritually, water relates to living in the present moment and the possibility of transformation that exists in every moment through trust in God. Just as water takes on the shape of whatever vessel it currently is in, living in the present moment means being able to accept and adapt to the current situation for what it is and to be open to the possibilities of what can and may come. Just as we speak about currents of water, we often refer to the present as the current moment—where the flow of life is right now.

Miriam was a model of what it looks like to live in the present moment. In fact, the source of her righteousness was her ability to live in the present moment through her complete trust in God. There were several episodes in her life, that we know about through the Torah text or through *midrashim* (oral traditions), that reveal her way of looking at the world and describe the choices that she made.

It might be easy to think that the few stories we have about Miriam were isolated incidents during her life. After all, we all have our moments of great strength. However, we need to re-member that Miriam's way of being in the world was so consis-tent and powerful that it translated into, and was manifested by, a constant flow of water for several million people for close to forty years while in the desert after leaving Egypt. That's a lot of water.

LIVING IN THE FLOW OF LIFE ...

When we come closer to our fountain, we notice that the water doesn't just stay within a pool. A stream of water flows out from the fountain's pool and meanders throughout the courtyard, symbolizing Miriam's gift for being able to live in the flow of life, regardless of circumstances. Listening to the sound of the water from the fountain rising, as well as hearing the stream trickling by, is calming and invigorating at the same time. Perhaps that is why the sound of water is always soothing: it is the sound of the present moment. It is as if God is calling us through nature to be in the flow of life and enter the centered state of being that living in the present moment creates. How did Miriam come to have this great gift of being able to live in the present moment with such trust in God?

It's all in her name ...

The name Miriam literally means "bitter waters"—"Mar Yam" or "Marim," meaning bitterness. Who would want a name like that, and even more, who would give a name like that to their child? Still, our tradition teaches us that our names are the calling of our soul and guide us in our lives. Our names can describe and give us insight into the mission, the challenges, and the gifts that we bring into this world. We know as a fact that Miriam—Mar Yam—was born into bitter times because she was born during the Jewish people's enslavement in Egypt. Living in the present moment requires us to acknowledge the situation we are in, not to deny it. However, acknowledging and accepting are two different things. Acknowledgment means to recognize and to know what is happening, while acceptance means to receive and somehow internalize the reality, making it a part of oneself. Miriam acknowledged the fact of the Jewish people's enslavement; she did not accept or live with an enslavement mentality as her reality.

MIRIAM— RISING TO THE CHALLENGE BY ANSWERING THE CALL OF HER SOUL ...

Once we acknowledge our situation or circumstances, then what? Miriam's name again helped her to recognize what her particular mission and challenges were. Because words written in the Torah only have consonants and no vowels, there are often different ways to read the same word. Miriam's name can also be read as *May-rim*, which means to elevate or to raise up. Miriam recognized that her mission was to elevate and raise up the Jewish people in their oppressive and demoralizing environment.

HOW DID MIRIAM'S NAME HELP HER FACE THE CHALLENGES OF ENSLAVEMENT?

We can look deeper into her name. Hidden in Miriam's name is the word "mayim," which means water. Water, and all that it symbolizes about being in the flow of life, is the gift that Miriam brought to face the challenges of enslavement. We'll come to understand more of the details soon, but water (in one form or another) is a recurring and underlying theme in several of the stories about Miriam. As we gaze at the majestic fountain, we are reminded that the way of water is the path of living in the present moment that will ultimately lift us up, as it did the Jewish people in Miriam's time.

MITZRAYIM—ACKNOWLEDGING OUR SITUATION BUT NOT ACCEPTING IT AS OUR REALITY ...

How do we live in the flow of the present moment when we are constricted and confined in enslavement, as we were in Egypt? It seems it wouldn't be possible. Miriam had a secret though, and it goes back to the idea that while we need to acknowledge our situation, we don't necessarily need to accept it as our static reality. We should look above and beyond what circumstances appear to be. Egypt was a real place, and the Jewish people's enslavement there was certainly a painfully real event. The bitter experience of Egypt is perfectly conveyed by the Hebrew word for Egypt: *"Mitzrayim,"* which means a narrow and constricted place. We can just about feel the harsh, almost choking feeling that the word conjures up. In spite of that, when we take a closer look at the Hebrew word *"Mitzrayim,"* guess what words we find hidden within it?

"Miriam," "mayrim," and "mayim" ...

מצרים Mitzrayim (Constricted)

מרים Miriam, Mayrim (Rising Up)

מים Mayim (Water)

"Miriam," *"mayrim"* (rising up), and *"mayim"* (water), are all in the word *"Mitzrayim."* Surprisingly, this word *"Mitzrayim,"* and all of the pain, sorrow, and oppression connected with it, appear to be changing before our eyes. The answer, even the antidote, to

Mitzrayim (constriction) is within the word itself. Miriam was the one who could help to raise the Jewish people through the path of water—living in the present moment—guiding them and helping them live a personal reality of redemption in the midst of their enslavement. Egypt is also used as a metaphor for times, places, and situations that are constricting and restricting. We should recognize, then, that every *mitzrayim* situation really contains three beacons within it: 1) the path of the present moment to transform our reality, 2) the role model of Miriam's wisdom and life experiences to guide and inspire us, and 3) the potential to be raised up and then elevated by the very circumstances we thought would crush us. What Miriam was able to teach the Jewish people is that it is possible to rise up and sail on, even in the turbulent waters of the present moment.

THE FLOW OF WATER PREVAILS ...

Our courtyard fountain pool is built of brick to symbolize the memory of the bricks the Jewish people were forced to make under the harsh oppression of Pharaoh's decrees in Egypt. As the fountain of water flows over the bricks and cascades down, we are reminded that in the end, water always prevails. Even in nature, the hardest rocks get etched and softened and even sometimes disintegrate from the constant flow of water.

The way of water is the path of living in the present moment, and its central focus in Miriam's Courtyard functions as a constant reminder that we can see, hear, and feel. We can now move toward the benches surrounding the fountain. At each bench, we will pause and share with you the extraordinary experiences that challenged Miriam. As we visit each bench, we invite you to appreciate the stories of how Miriam acknowledged the bitter challenges of the Jewish people's lives, but chose to live her life as someone uplifted rather than bitter.

THE FIRST BENCH:
LIVING WITH A VISION

*"I am sure that Pharaoh's edict will soon be
withdrawn, while your decree will endure."*

*—Miriam, in response to her
father (Midrash Shemot Rabba)*

As we approach our first bench, we see the above quote is engraved on it. This quote captures the essence of the story that we are about to relate.

AN EDICT IS GIVEN
BUT A CHOICE IS MADE ...

Pharaoh, fearful that a Jewish boy would grow up and overthrow him, issued a decree against the Jewish people during their enslavement in Egypt: all newborn Jewish boys were to be drowned in the Nile River. The righteous leader of the generation and head of the Sanhedrin (Jewish Court) at that time was Amram from the tribe of Levi. When Pharaoh issued this decree, Amram had two children, Miriam and Aaron. When Amram heard that all newborn males were doomed to extermination, he reasoned, "Why should we have more children, only to see them slaughtered?" He therefore decided to divorce his wife, Yocheved, in order to prevent more children from being born. Since he was the leader of the community, all the other Jewish men followed his lead and also separated from their wives. Miriam, a child of just eight years old at the time, argued with her father. "Your decision is harsher than that of the king," she said. "While Pharaoh's law affects only male children, with your decision, you are preventing the birth of both boys and girls. And I am sure that Pharaoh's edict will soon be withdrawn, while your decision will endure." Amram acknowledged the force of Miriam's arguments. He decided that he and his wife should reunite in a very public way so that the entire community would follow their example, which they did. Six months later, Yocheved gave birth to Moses, the future leader and redeemer of the Jewish people.

A RATIONAL CHOICE BASED ON A PREMISE OF FAITH ...

Amram's original decision to separate from his wife and avoid having any more children was a completely logical one that reflected a reasonable sense of concern about the danger of Jewish life in Egypt. It certainly seems rational to decide to not bring children into the world if you are certain they are going to be killed. Some people today don't even want to bring children into the world when life gets a little tough. Miriam saw things differently. She knew that Amram's plan would have eventually destroyed the Jewish people. Life is sometimes overwhelmingly painful, but we make it worse when we make choices that cut off all hope for the future and, in fact, make the desired future even more remote.

Something else was also abundantly clear to Miriam. Her father's decision assumed that Pharaoh's decree would be in place forevermore, so the Jewish people were doomed. But Pharaoh was a finite human being. He may have thought he was a god and tried to play God, but he was a mere human and could not live forever. Decrees, even harsh ones, come and go. But every life not brought into this world would have had eternal consequences. The Jewish people would never be able to go back and have the children they could have had or build the nation they eventually built. It was painful enough that Pharaoh's decrees caused so much suffering. The Jewish people didn't need to intensify their suffering by reacting to the decree rather than to God's promise.

LIVING IN TRUST WITH A FAITHFUL VISION OF REALITY ...

Miriam trusted in God's promise of redemption from Egypt, and she put her faith in, and based her choices on, trust. She refused to be influenced and misdirected by Pharaoh's attempt to control the destiny of the Jewish people. Miriam was not willing to make choices based on Pharaoh's twisted *version* of reality. She was aligned with and encouraged a faithful *vision* of reality—God's promised redemption. The difficult and dangerous choices that she made and advocated were consistent with her vision. Some of Miriam's choices might have looked irrational or frightening to someone with a different perspective, but to Miriam, they were the most rational choices of all. Through her vision and trust in God's promise of redemption, Miriam inspired her father and the Jewish people to redirect their efforts—to have children and create the families that would build the future Jewish nation.

HOW TO BE FREE IN CAPTIVITY ...

It's easy and understandable to be scared when someone or something has so much power to hurt us, like Pharaoh. Nevertheless, we are never completely helpless or hopeless. We are always free, at least, to choose our response to any given situation. When we acknowledge the particular circumstances in which we happen to find ourselves, we can recognize the facts and what options we have. Then we can make our choices. However, looking only at certain facts doesn't necessarily give us an accurate picture of reality. Facts don't exist in a vacuum. There is always a context to any situation. When we accept the mindset and thinking of whomever or whatever is oppressing us as being *true*, we attach ourselves to the oppressor's version of reality. We enter into their context and framework. Accepting this context distorts our perception of reality and limits our recognition of what choices we have and what does lie within our power to do. When we sacrifice our vision, we lose the ability to free ourselves from the construct of a reality being imposed on us. Ultimately, that disempowers and imprisons us.

Viktor Frankl, in *Man's Search for Meaning*, relates his experience being a prisoner in a Nazi concentration camp. Despite the Nazis' relentless, barbaric, and horrifying attempts to dehumanize their prisoners and their success in murdering millions,

Viktor Frankl had the wisdom to recognize that the Nazis could not control *his* vision of *his* humanity with their distorted version of reality. This gave him incredible strength and courage to retain his humanity and dignity, regardless of what they did to his body, and to make choices that seemed impossible in the conditions under which he was forced to live.

Making choices in the present moment with a clear vision of reality, even if that reality seems obscured and distant, also allows us to see things for what they are without being immobilized by additional fear. The truth is that in Nazi Germany, like in Egypt, the leaders had the power to hurt us and kill us. We would have given them even more power if we had accepted their version of reality and internalized their warped perspective that defined us as worthless victims.

BREAKING DOWN THE PYRAMID OF PAIN ...

Egypt was the superpower of its time. When we think of the symbol of Egypt, most of us think of the pyramids—massive, heavy, imposing structures that were built as much for self-glorification as for their architectural, agricultural, and religious purposes. Pyramids speak of strength, power, and eternity. How dare someone like little Miriam speak up and challenge all that Pharaoh and Egypt symbolized? She actually knocked Pharaoh and Egypt down to size by reminding her father, Amram, that while Pharaoh could kill us and hurt us, he was not the ultimate power, he wasn't a god, and he wouldn't last forever. In Miriam's time, a finite human being did appear to have the power to hurt and kill

half of our children if he found them. We didn't know how successful he would be or how long his decree would last. Should we
have turned our lives upside down because of him? Miriam, like
Viktor Frankel, said, "No."

Our challenge is to have a vision of reality that is true and
firm, so that the harsh and pressing presence of a warped and cruel situation doesn't distort our own sense of what is happening,
leading us to overreact and under-respond. Difficult situations
are challenging enough without our heaping more rocks and
stones onto the pyramid of pain. Living in the present moment
doesn't mean that we'll always perceive life as being sweet in every situation; it means that we'll see the truth of the moment and
understand what choices we really have.

THE SECOND BENCH:
WAITING AND WATCHING
AT THE WATER'S EDGE

"His sister stationed herself at a distance to know what would be done with him." – Exodus 2:4

We walk quietly to the next bench and read the quote above, which describes Miriam's experience when her brother Moses was an infant. We hear the sound of water trickling through the courtyard's meandering stream. We stand and watch it, and imagine what Miriam did thousands of years ago when she stood by the Nile River after her baby brother Moses was placed in a reed basket and sent floating down the river. Yocheved, Moses' mother, fearful of Pharaoh's death decree against newborn Jewish baby boys and the inevitable discovery of Moses' birth, had hidden him in a basket and put him into the river. According to the *Midrash* (rabbinic narratives), Yocheved hoped that putting Moses in the water would confuse Pharaoh's magicians and, thinking that Moses had disappeared and presumably drowned, they would stop looking for him. Miriam was the only one who waited and watched by the water's edge to see what would happen to her brother.

WAITING AND WATCHING ...

On the surface, waiting and watching don't seem to have much to do with living in the present moment. Miriam didn't appear to be doing anything. She was standing there. However, two strong and specific words used in the Torah hint that there was more going on than simply standing and looking. When we read, "His sister stationed herself at a distance to know what would be done with him," (Exodus 2:4), we notice that the text says she "stationed herself," like a guard or a sentry or a person on a mission. Her goal wasn't to *gawk* at what was happening, but rather to *know* what was happening so that she could plan her actions. There was something different about Miriam's waiting and watching. She was waiting expectantly and watching carefully. She trusted that whatever happened next was the next step in the redemptive process unfolding; she was watching to see what opportunities were being presented right then in the events at hand. This kind of waiting and watching were both profound demonstrations of living in the present moment with deep trust and using the gifts of imagination and free choice in a way that allowed her to stay focused.

CLARITY OF VISION ...

Miriam was not standing by passively, paralyzed with fear. She was poised and ready to take the next step when it became clear. Because she held a vision of God's promised redemption and recognized that redemption is a process, Miriam knew that every moment brought redemption one step closer. When Miriam stood at the water's edge, she recognized that she was standing on the edge of change and at any moment something significant could happen. She stood with heightened awareness and was prepared to see miracles come from unexpected places and from unexpected people. It was her clarity of vision that allowed her to be completely present in the moment. We can trust that there is a process, whether there are difficult or painful situations within the process or not. That is all part of the overall plan and design for Creation and its ultimate purpose and completion. If everything on the grand scale is meaningful, then each individual part is also meaningful and purposeful, even if it is difficult or painful at the moment. This is the trust Miriam had and we can cultivate it as well.

BATYA'S RESPONSE ...

And what *did* happen? Pharaoh's daughter Batya, bathing in the Nile, saw the baby Moses and reached out to bring him to shore and into her arms. At that point, Miriam could have entirely and justifiably panicked. Here was the woman whose father's decree of death caused Moses to be in the Nile in the first place, reaching for him. What a disaster! *Would she turn him in? Would she kill him herself? What could be worse?* If Miriam had been in a state of panic, caused by using her imagination to conjure up fears of disaster, she might have rushed over to Batya, grabbed Moses from her, and caused a major incident, creating a barrier to what was supposed to unfold next.

We see that Miriam didn't panic at all. In fact, she was completely calm. She saw the way Batya handled Moses—gently and with affection, even though Batya recognized from Moses's circumcision that he was a Jewish baby. Miriam also saw that Batya was not hurting Moses; in fact, she appeared to be protecting him. Batya was clearly, though surprisingly, the perfect person to have found Moses. What could have been better?

WHAT'S THE NEXT BEST STEP?

Miriam used her imagination to perceive other possibilities, rather than just fearful ones. She saw that the next step was to help Batya keep Moses. Batya now needed a way to feed this baby. First things first. Moses was the future redeemer of the Jewish people, but right then, he was a hungry infant. Miriam went to Pharaoh's daughter and asked, "Shall I go and summon for you a wet nurse from the Hebrew women, who will nurse the boy for you?" (Exodus 2:7). Batya agreed and Miriam went to get her (and Moses's) own mother, Yocheved, to nurse Moses. Pharaoh's daughter said to Yocheved, "Take this boy and nurse him for me, and I will give you your pay." (Exodus 2:9.)

FOCUSING ON REDEMPTION ...

Moses grew up and Yocheved took him back to Batya, Pharoah's daughter, and "he was a son to her." (Exodus 2: 9–10). It was Moses's unique position of being Jewish and a member of the royal household that put him in place to later emerge as the leader and redeemer of the Jewish people. Even if Yocheved, Amram, and Miriam had thought for weeks on end about how they could save

Moses from death, they would never have conceived of this scenario that, in the end, proved to be exactly what needed to happen to pave the way for the redemption of the Jewish people and the exodus from Egypt. Keeping our imaginations focused on a redemptive and positive vision, instead of fearful projections, opens up possibilities and outcomes that we could not have imagined.

KEEPING YOUR HEAD UP ...

We now have more appreciation for the significance of Miriam's waiting and watching, and how developing these two qualities can help make miraculous things happen. We see how Miriam kept her "head up" and helped transform her brother's bitter situation, of drifting on the Nile with a death decree hanging over him, to a promising one where he was taken in and protected by Pharaoh's daughter herself. The water, the *mayim*, that could have drowned Moses, instead delivered him to safety. Miriam, truly being in the flow of the present moment, made the choices that brought deliverance one step closer.

Everything that Miriam did and said can guide us on our own path of redemption. The precarious situation of Moses being put into the Nile symbolizes how we can often feel in times of trouble where we feel out of control and on the verge of some sort of disaster. Moses's basket floating in the Nile symbolized being adrift with no knowledge of what's going to happen next. Being a baby in the Nile suggested the vulnerability and danger that we feel.

On the verge of change ...

But Miriam being at the water's edge helps us in recognizing that the only thing we know for sure is that we are on the verge of change. We don't really know what lies ahead. In truth, anything is possible at any moment. Although most of us prefer the secure feeling of being on firm ground, rather than drifting to who-knows-where, for someone who knows how to swim, being at the water's edge is exciting and presents all sorts of opportunities. For someone who doesn't know how to swim, flowing water can look daunting and frightening.

Miriam never literally jumped into the water to start swimming, but she kept her head up spiritually through the situation with grace and poise. Her underlying source of strength was her trust in God's promise of eventual redemption of the Jewish people from slavery in Egypt. (It would be eighty years later that Moses, as a grown man, would lead the Jewish people in the Exodus from Egypt.) The exodus from Egypt is considered to be a model for all redemptions—personal, communal, and universal.

For humans, our underlying source of strength is the trust that God has created a purposeful world and life is unfolding and moving persistently, if slowly, toward God's ultimate goal. Since the entire Creation is purposeful at the macrocosmic level, it is consistent to reason that it is also purposeful at the personal, microcosmic level. The challenge is recognizing the reality that we are constantly being given moments—both pleasant and painful—to make meaningful choices in furtherance of God's purpose for us and for all of Creation. Understanding this, and integrating it into our hearts and minds, is the essence of living in the present moment. Miriam teaches us how to make the most of painful moments, which are also part of the redemptive process.

STANDING AT THE EDGE ...

Miriam's standing and waiting teaches us that there are times when it is important to wait to see what is going to happen next, rather than rushing in panic-stricken because we feel that we have to do something immediately. Just as a camera can capture a moment when a person has an awful expression that doesn't reflect how the person really looks, if we snap the picture of a situation prematurely, we can come to the wrong conclusion about the flow of events and about what is going to, or could, happen next. We want our perspective of life to resemble an ongoing movie rather than a series of disjointed, individual photos.

Miriam's waiting also tells us that she wasn't just waiting for any random thing to happen, but that she was waiting for the next step toward redemption to present itself. Her trust helped her wait for something that was truly good, even though the situation might not have looked at all promising (initially or superficially). How often do opportunities come our way to help us through difficult situations, but we fail to recognize them because they're packaged in an unexpected or challenging way? When we trust that these opportunities are there, and are willing to wait for the moments to unfold, the amount of potential flowing our way will surprise us.

Miriam's waiting was watchful and attentive, and we can learn from her approach and experience. We need to be careful as we watch a situation because our perceptions are often so biased that we can't tell what is really going on. We may not do it intentional-ly, but how often do we see what we want to see, what we thought we'd see, or what we were afraid we'd see, rather than what was actually happening? Our minds, in their effort to "protect" us, put filters on what we see so that we can deal with all of the in-put that is bombarding us constantly. That is helpful in many circumstances because it's very tiring to evaluate every moment as a brand-new moment with infinite potential at all times. Most of our filters, however, come from scripts that help us determine quickly what is happening. If a new situation has any features of a previous situation, we judge it to be the same and we've got our response all ready to go. However, this protective mechanism isn't always in our best interest because it can leave us stuck and oblivious to the potential in a new situation.

WHAT HELPED MIRIAM SEE SO CLEARLY?

Miriam was able to see clearly because she trusted the potential that lies in every situation, unfettered by past patterns or events or fearful predictions of the future. Miriam's watching teaches us not to project a script onto what we see, a script that biases our perception of what is happening in the here and now. The Torah text specifically says that "she stationed herself at a distance to know what would be done with him (Moses)." (Exodus 2:4). The implication is that by stationing herself a bit of a distance away, she could gain perspective and wait to know what her next action should be. She didn't make biased judgments or offer predictions. She was waiting to know—to see clearly how people were behav-ing and to perceive the subtleties of the situation. Because not knowing feels so uncomfortable, we are often more emotionally at ease when we jump to conclusions—even when they are bad ones—rather than patiently waiting to see what the new reality is.

When we were children, we were taught that "patience is a virtue," and (for most of us) that meant learning to wait, squirming, until it was our turn at a game, for an acceptance letter from college, or for the results of a test. As adults, we can appreciate that patience is a virtue because it recognizes that things happen one step at a time and we can't rush the process of life unfolding. In fact, every step along the way is necessary and important. We're not just biding our time until the final step occurs.

The truth of this is brought to life for us in a story about a butterfly that is told by a great rabbi, who shared this message with his young student. The story was retold by Sender Rothman in an article titled, "The Burden and the Butterfly."

A man once noticed a butterfly cocoon in his yard. He was intrigued by it and wanted to watch for the butterfly that would soon emerge. A few days went by and the man was excited to see a small opening in the cocoon. He patiently waited for the butterfly to emerge. Initially, the butterfly pushed its head through the opening. Thinking that the butterfly would soon be free, the man was distressed to see that the butterfly, in fact, was struggling and not seeming to make any further progress. The man, fearing the butterfly would not survive the struggle, decided to help it by using scissors to open the cocoon. After the man carefully opened the cocoon, the butterfly did emerge, and the man thought he was successful. But he soon realized there was something wrong. The butterfly had shriveled wings and an enlarged body and didn't seem to be moving in the right way. Hoping the situation would improve and the butterfly would fly away, he waited, but nothing changed. Sadly, the butterfly never did improve and spent its life crawling, with a swollen body and shriveled wings. What the man didn't realize was that the struggle to emerge from the cocoon was the precise process needed for the fluid from the butterfly's body to move into its shriveled wings, opening them up so that the butterfly could soar.

The butterfly's struggle is like those in our own lives. There are struggles God has designed for us and given to us to help us grow and soar. Keeping the story of this butterfly in mind can help us value and respect the struggles we have and recognize they do have the potential to bring us to new heights.

Miriam's actions with Pharaoh's daughter reflected her realization that redemption happens one step at a time and that often the next step is not something dramatic or glamorous, but rather something as critical, but mundane, as getting a baby something to eat. It's so easy to overlook these necessary steps along the way of our life. In especially difficult or painful moments, we just want the difficulty to end, rather than recognizing that we have been presented with a meaningful opportunity and need to act.

We can find small examples of impatience with the process in the physical realm of our daily lives. Isn't it interesting to watch commercials about over-the-counter medicines that will get you back to work, school, and play while you are still sick with a bad cold or the flu? Who says that's the right response? Maybe we're supposed to be patient with the process of being a patient and stay home, read, sleep, and let our bodies deal with the illness. Many doctors are now telling patients that in certain situations it is better to let the fever stay and not try to get it to go away because the fever itself helps the body fight the infection. This is not a negative statement about medications; it is an observation about our culture's lack of patience with everything, especially discomfort and other painful situations. A Jewish equivalent would be the process of sitting *shiva*, the seven-day mourning period after the death of a close relative. In our society, people believe they are supposed to "get over" their pain and move on. We see, though, that sitting *shiva*, and all the rituals involved with it, shows us that patience with the process of openly dealing with pain lets us begin healing.

LIVING DAY TO DAY WITH A VISION OF REDEMPTION ...

Miriam lived her life with a clear and expansive vision of redemption for the Jewish people. She also had the ability to take one small step at a time toward that vision. The combination of her future perspective and her ability to recognize and appreciate the potential of small steps allowed Miriam to live every moment completely aware of the pull toward redemption and make choices consistent with that vision. We'll see in another part of Miriam's Courtyard that some of these choices seemed irrational to others, and yet they were entirely consistent with her vision. This state of mind enabled her to be joyful, even in difficult moments, because the light of future redemption shined brightly and seemed very close to her all the time. Most of us suffer because we haven't yet learned Miriam's lesson. We often have no vision at all or our vision seems so distant and clouded that it doesn't have any reality to it. We spend our time hoping things will change, but we don't see how our small efforts and actions can make a difference. We think that because ultimate redemption lies in a future that is so far off, we can't see or experience the process of it gradually unfolding in the here and now. This narrow and constrained view of life is its own form of emotional and mental enslavement.

Even though we usually focus on Moses's role as leader and redeemer of the Jewish people from Egypt, the prophet Micah reminds us that Miriam (and Aaron too) were part of the redemption process. Miriam's gift to the Jewish people then, and to us now, is to teach us how to break the chains of an enslaved way of thinking and to keep our vision present in the everyday moments of our lives. Whether the times seem bitter or sweet, we have to make choices that bring our personal lives, as well as the lives of our people, closer to complete fulfillment. We often have opportunities to stand at the water's edge, just as Miriam did, waiting and watching—poised but not paralyzed—to see what is unfolding in our lives and what the next small, but significant, step is that we can take.

Let's continue on to the next bench ...

THE THIRD BENCH:
MIDWIFING MIRACLES

*"And God benefited the midwives—and the people
increased and became very strong. And it was because the
midwives awed God that He made them houses."*

– Exodus 1:20

As you can see by the quote on this next bench, we're now
going to focus on the amazing leadership that Miriam displayed
through her gift as a midwife to the Jewish women in Egypt and
how she encouraged these women to live in the present moment
with strength and trust.

Most leaders of nations lead their people *en masse*. Their focus
and concern aren't necessarily on individuals. However, nations
must be built before they can be led. Building, unlike leading,
is done one person at a time. Miriam was a builder. She led the
building of the House of Israel, the nation that God promised to
redeem from slavery in Egypt. Her leadership was one-on-one
and came to the Jewish women through her gift of being their
midwife. Helping women bring their children into the world at
any time is a deeply interpersonal and precious experience. Being
a midwife and being willing to give birth when there is a death

decree against all newborn males is an act of utmost heroic courage. Miriam and her mother, Yocheved, were under direct orders from Pharaoh to kill all of the newborn males, and they refused to do it. Under those threatening circumstances, to consciously choose birth intensified and also verified the women's vision of a Jewish nation being born and built. Each new child was a living symbol of trust in God's promise of redemption.

Just as Holocaust survivors went on to have families, those children were more than the ordinary miracle of babies being born; they were a message of hope and trust and a strong statement against the decree of death.

SPIRITUAL STRENGTH COMES FROM BEING IN THE PRESENT MOMENT ...

The spiritual strength that went into the conception, labor, and delivery of the children born in Egypt seems to have had a direct impact on them—both physically and spiritually. As the Torah teaches us, God benefited the midwives and the people multiplied and became very strong because of their awe of God. It does not say that the people became strong because the midwives were technical experts. The babies grew and became people with powerful physical strength built upon the deep spiritual strength and trust in God of their mothers and midwives. Miriam and her mother, Yocheved, strengthened the women's spirits and encouraged them to be attuned to the incredible potential that lay within each of them to build the Jewish nation through the Jewish children to whom they would give birth.

It is no surprise to learn that the word for children in Hebrew is "banim," which is related to the word "bonim," meaning "builders." When we realize that close connection, we appreciate that the spiritual strength of the children banim (children) born from their mothers' faith created the bonim (builders) needed to lay the firm foundation for the holy nation that God would redeem in the future.

LIVING WITH VISION AND TRUSTING THE MOMENT ...

· The breaking of each woman's water brought forth the birth of a new child, and Miriam, the woman of water, was there to help it happen. We can just imagine the tears of joy, relief, and hopefulness that flowed as mother and midwife swaddled and cuddled each tiny baby who represented trust in the future and willingness to live in the difficult and painful present with that vision of the future.

What a lesson to be learned. Everything surrounding birth speaks to us about living in the present moment and wisdom for life. From the very beginning, a woman is not in control of the process of her child being formed within her. She must stay in the flow of the pregnancy. She can neither speed it up or slow it down. She must trust the moment. Trusting the birth process shows us that we can trust God to deliver us and redeem us, both as individuals and as a people.

Trust within the process ...

In addition to the power of giving birth, where each delivery in Egypt defied the decree of death, the entire birth process could be experienced as a living metaphor and reminder of the Jewish people's journey from enslavement to redemption. Even the idea that pregnancy is a process—one that takes a certain amount of time—furthers our understanding of patience. Especially in today's world, where everything is measured in seconds, the ability to stay with a process that takes time challenges us. We become impatient when viewing our personal lives, let alone the destiny of humanity, as requiring time to unfold. It is difficult for us to realize that the process creates the results we hope for and is not just an amount of time to be endured or escaped from. For all of our technological progress, a full-term pregnancy is still nine months.

The dimension of forty in time and space ...

A full-term pregnancy is also counted in weeks: forty weeks. In our tradition, the number forty is always connected to the idea of transformation. Change occurs in the dimensions of time and space. Time and space are not a neutral backdrop to what is going on in our lives but instead are essential ingredients. There is an interrelationship between time, space, and specific experiences: each is necessary for us to move from one state of being to another—to truly transform. We're familiar with some other forties in the Torah: the forty days and nights of rain during Noah's Flood, the forty days and nights that Moses spends on top of Mt. Sinai, the forty days the spies spend in the Land of Israel, and the forty years that the Jewish people spend in the Midbar (the desert) after leaving Egypt.

The forty-year journey of the Jewish people in the desert mirrors the forty-week pregnancy that results in the miracle of a new human being. Through this forty-year gestation period in the desert, the Jews were transformed from released slaves burdened by their oppression to free partners with God who trusted the potential of their still unknown future in the Land of Israel. Just as certain parts of the baby develop at different stages of a pregnancy, the Jewish people were given specific experiences at different encampments during their forty years to enable them to change and become "full-term."

THE HIDDEN PROCESS OF REDEMPTION ...

Our impatience with the process of transformation and change also comes from the reality that we can't detect much of the process as it is occurring. Just because we can't see something changing, doesn't mean that it isn't. Pregnancy reminds us of this too. A pregnant woman knows that even before she starts "to show," tremendous growth and change are underway. In fact, the most miraculous event—conception—happens without any awareness on our part. Miriam knew and reminded the women that this aspect of concealment was also true of the Jewish people's promised redemption and that God was setting the stage in hidden ways for their birth as a nation. Delivery and deliverance—of their child and their nation—would happen *b'sha'ah tovah* (at a good time).

BIRTHING CAN BE DIFFICULT
AND PAINFUL ...

As a baby approaches its time of delivery, it gets more cramped and uncomfortable in the womb. The very place of growth and nurturing becomes stifling just before birth. Egypt is often described in a similar way.

The Hebrew for Egypt is Mitzrayim, which means narrow and constricted, and is a vivid description of what that place was and what the Jews' experience there was all about. Mitzrayim hints at both the physical and spiritual challenges that oppressed and molded the Jewish people for 210 years. We can imagine Miriam reassuring the Jewish women that the final difficult days of pregnancy and harsh pains of labor were the very signals that birth was near and that their own situation as a people was in the same phase. It is always the most difficult just before the end, and it is so easy to give up. Luckily, in birth, the mother has little choice about going through labor and delivery. She, like the child she carries, is swept up in the most primal process—bringing new life into the world.

After witnessing the baby emerging from the narrow birth canal, Miriam might also have encouraged the new mother that the Jewish people would also emerge from Mitzrayim (Egypt)—their narrow place and that we needed to trust God as the midwife who would deliver us safely.

Our natural inclination is to resist and try to avoid any situation—physical or emotional—that feels confining, cramped, or oppressive. Generally, this is a good idea. There are, however, some situations that cannot be changed immediately, and we must live with the circumstances. Beyond just trying to endure them, we have another path in front of us. Each of us is pregnant with potential. We can consider that this time or place or situation is a labor and delivery room for us, and we can be open to the possibility that we need to refine or squeeze that potential out of us and that we have a chance to give birth to a new version of ourselves through the hardship we are experiencing.

THE STRUGGLE TO FLY ...

The story of the "Burden and the Butterfly," which we related earlier, recounts that the butterfly's struggle to get out of the cocoon was necessary to strengthen its wings and allow it to fly successfully. We are like the butterfly. Our struggles and challenges, while uncomfortable, are developmental cocoons that are necessary for our own process of change and growth. Only through those struggles can we emerge stronger and soar to new heights.

A PREGNANCY MINDSET ...

Perhaps God created the discomfort of human pregnancy—for the mother and possibly the child too—to remind us that growth and redemption are difficult. As a baby grows in utero, it pulls and stretches the mother. Pregnancy tends to cramp our style, and we rarely get to choose the particulars involved with it. In the end though, it is the whole process that, with all its discomfort, brings new birth. What a shame it would be if we misread the situation. What if the baby tried to get out of its cramped space before its time? What if the mother decided she was too tired of having sore feet and heartburn and wearing big clothes? What if, at moments of discomfort, difficulty, or despair, we gave up hope? At challenging moments in our own lives, we can picture Miriam standing by our side, softly whispering words of encouragement, soothing our pain and panic with practiced words of wisdom. Miriam's lessons can guide and strengthen us to fully be in each moment we're in, reminding us where we've been and where we are going and to trust that God will help us to get there. By keeping Miriam in mind, she can inspire us as an ever-present midwife, helping us to continually rebirth ourselves.

Miriam's leadership of the Jewish people extended to all of the Jewish women, as we'll see at our next bench ...

THE FOURTH BENCH: FROM
TOURNIQUETS TO TAMBOURINES

"Miriam the Prophetess, the sister of Aaron, took her timbrel (drum) in her hand and all the women went forth after her with drums and with dances. Miriam spoke up to them, "Sing to Hashem for He is exalted above the arrogant, having hurled horse with its rider into the sea."

– Exodus 15:20–21

This quote from the Torah, inscribed on our fourth bench, describes what happened after the Jewish people left Egypt and experienced the miracle of the Sea splitting for them as the Egyptians relentlessly pursued them.

Knowing that Miriam had her timbrel in hand at that time, or it was easily accessible before leaving Egypt during the Exodus, is inspiring. It would be easy to look at the impending situation very differently. Heading into the unknown after 210 years of Egyptian slavery could have been very frightening. Was there more danger ahead? How many of us would have been more likely to pack tourniquets rather than timbrels—anticipating more pain and suffering, rather than perceiving ourselves in the middle of redemption? Unfortunately, we are taught to prepare for disasters rather than deliverance.

EXPECTING THE BEST ...

Our expectations create a certain mindset. Even when packing for a trip, we tend to focus on being ready for something to go wrong and for situations not to work out. So, we bring our toothbrush in our carry-on in case the airline loses our luggage. We carry a first-aid kit when we go on a hike, in case someone falls. These are all necessary and prudent precautions, but what about remembering to take camera batteries and chargers because we anticipate there will be great photo opportunities? Or what about taking a journal because we know we'll want to record special moments from our trip? Would we go so far as to bring extra food because we're hoping that we'll meet someone new whom we'll want to include in one of our meals?

The details may vary, but at the core is a way of living with the trust that good things—even great things—are not only in store for us but are in the process of becoming a reality. We should want to be ready for them. In fact, being ready for them has the potential effect of hastening their occurrence. Preparing is different than waiting, though sometimes only in subtle ways. Although 210 years had passed while the Jewish people were enslaved in Egypt, Miriam did not sit and wait for redemption to happen. According to our Midrash, Miriam had spent years lifting the women's spirits, helping them maintain trust in God's promise of redemption, and inspiring them to act on their trust by making redemptive choices in the midst of their suffering. Miriam encouraged the women to continue having children and to focus on building the Jewish people. Not only was this an act of defiance against Pharaoh; it was an act of trust that helped pave the way for redemption to occur.

READY TO SING ...

The vision of redemption that Miriam trusted in and prepared the women for finally came. After the Exodus from Egypt, the entire Jewish nation crossed the Sea that God split miraculously. The Egyptians who had been pursuing them were killed, and the Jewish people arrived safely on the other side. The response to this miracle was that everyone sang out in joyful praise and thanksgiving. The men sang first, and then Miriam and the women responded. What is interesting is that the words Miriam said were identical to what the men had already sung. It could seem that Miriam and the women's contribution was redundant. However, what makes all the difference is that only the women sang with the timbrels they had brought with them from Egypt, demonstrating their faith and trust that redemption was within reach. They were ready to sing and prepared to rejoice.

Miriam felt her trust in God so deeply, and lived it so openly, that she didn't have a doubt that redemption would come. Even more, in the midst of the enslavement, she perceived redemption unfolding. We tend to compartmentalize life—this is the "bad" part and this is the "good" part. Miriam's gift is to lift the good out of the bad until all that is left is the good. Miriam truly lived up to her name: she took every opportunity to focus on taking positive steps—large and small—simultaneously, while living in the midst of the bitterness around her. Yes, the waters are bitter but yes, with trust in God, we can lift ourselves up from the bitterness. For Miriam, the salvation at the Sea was a logical and anticipated conclusion to the whole process, rather than a surprise ending.

Maybe we should each carry at least a figurative tiny timbrel with us wherever we go, as a reminder that life is always moving toward ultimate completion and redemption. We have choices to make along the way that can move us there more quickly and powerfully. It is amazing what can happen when we adopt Miriam's approach and how many tiny miracles we can help create to sing about at the end of the day.

MOVING FROM MIRIAM'S COURTYARD INTO THE HOUSE OF THE PRESENT MOMENT ...

Miriam's stories are compelling and are meant to inspire us. After taking in so many details of her experiences, we want to learn more about how we, too, can live in the present moment. One doesn't wake up one day and just announce, "Today I'm going to live in the present moment." That would be a great declaration, but the chances of success are quite small. Just as Miriam's life stories show that her ability to live in the present moment was a lifelong way of being in the world, we also need to know how to make living in the present moment a way of life. How do we get started? Is there some way to take small steps and to practice? Is there a place we could go to learn and explore more about how to live in this heightened state of awareness as Miriam did? Yes, there is, and that's what the rest of this book is about. There is a Divine Design for living that the House of the Present Moment offers us. Now that we've been introduced to Miriam as the model of what living in the present moment looks like, let's move into the house in which she would be very comfortable living.

When we first entered Miriam's Courtyard, we saw gracefully arched doorways. Now we're going to step into our House of the Present Moment through the archways, and we'll see that they lead into the very kind of place for which we're searching. The archways will take us into unique rooms, specifically designed to help us discover multiple ways to practice and cultivate the skills and strategies needed to live a more fulfilling life in the present moment. Each room is built with four inviting alcoves, with comfortable places to sit within each one. Each alcove will entice us to come a little closer and experience the wisdom and real-life lessons we can learn within their divinely designed space.

It is in these alcoves that we invite you to stop and take some time to reflect on the insights and messages each has to offer. Although this book is written in a linear format and the pages go from Page 1 to the end, we want to remind you that these rooms and alcoves in our House of the Present Moment are each places of engagement where you can linger in areas that resonate more deeply with your life situation, and to which you can later come back and spend more time to absorb more. As you are the person who has the power to direct your life and to build your own House of the Present, take your time and take full advantage of each room in this house. Let the messages you find the most meaningful sink in.

Let's begin by going in through the first archway and experiencing a room that is going to look and feel surprisingly different, while comfortably familiar as well.

II.

Shabbat Room

INTRODUCTION

AS WE WALK THROUGH THE FIRST ARCH we come to a room with a welcoming sign hanging over the entry: *Shabbat Shalom* (a peaceful, harmonious, and complete Sabbath). This is the Shabbat room, a room that represents both a time and a place to deeply experience living in the present moment. Shabbat is the foundation, and therefore the most important holiday and celebration we have. It is the core of Jewish life and living.

Shabbat generates a wealth of spiritual richness. We access abundant gifts that the spiritual world offers us by using ordinary physical objects. With those objects and the rituals associated with them, we create the atmosphere of our Shabbat experience.

Shabbat is ushered in with the lighting of candles. It is followed by the reciting of *Kiddush*, the blessing over a full cup of wine, which sanctifies the day of Shabbat. Kiddush is, in turn, followed by the blessing over two loaves of challah, bread used especially for Shabbat and other holidays. Twenty-five hours later, on Saturday night, after three stars appear, we escort the Shabbat out with the Havdalah ceremony that uses flame, wine, and sweet-smelling spices. Throughout Shabbat we will see, feel, taste, and even smell the present moment, allowing us to experience firsthand the joy and peacefulness created in our hearts and souls. Designed to be the "longest" day of the week, this sensory-rich day is the pulsating heart of Jewish life, and each aspect of it can be accessed to help us on our life's journey of living deeply in the present moment.

How helpful it is to know that there is a day every single week designated and given to us as a gift for this purpose. There is no need to book a room at a meditative spa. We already have a standing reservation at this five-star spiritual retreat in time called "Shabbat." We just need to be sure not to cancel our reservation or fail to show up.

So, we'll now enter the first alcove, where two candles in tall silver candlesticks are flickering in the soft sunlight that gently bathes the sky just before sunset.

SHABBAT CANDLES: THE SPIRITUAL LIGHT OF CREATION

We usher in Shabbat with the lighting of candles, and as we enter the first alcove we see the pair of candles glowing, gracing a lace-covered table and casting a luminous, yet soft, light. We slow down and maybe even sigh. It is so peaceful.

It is intriguing that no matter how advanced we become in technology, there is something compelling about candlelight. It doesn't seem to matter what kind of artificial lighting is available, actual candlelight conveys a special message. Perhaps it is because a flame creates both heat and light and because a candle's flicker manages to soften the environment around us and caress our eyes. Since our eyes are the windows to our souls, it is as if the candlelight is able to penetrate our very soul. In many situations, candles can create this effect. What is different about Shabbat candles?

One of the reasons we light Shabbat candles is to remind ourselves of the spiritual light that was created and visible at the beginning of Creation, and the harmony and tranquility of the Garden of Eden. Shabbat is called a "version of the world to come" and anticipates being in the Garden of Eden once more. The Garden brings to mind that time and place where and when the purpose of Creation was clear and distractions were few. It is almost impossible to hang onto this vision day in and day out. One of the obstacles to keeping the Garden as an active memory and a guide to living in the present moment is that most of the time our senses are overloaded: we can't define or determine exactly what is going on around us. Shabbat candles bring us pleasure at the physical level, but they also bring us spiritual joy because they remind us to stop and reflect on where we came from at the very beginning—the Garden—and what our ultimate destination is—back to the Garden, to the place where there is clarity and harmony.

The light of the Shabbat candles is not meant to create a romantic atmosphere. We light our Shabbat candles in a room that is already well illuminated. You might ask, "If the room is already lit, what is the added benefit of Shabbat candles?" Physical light is always associated with spiritual light, and a flame is also compared to the *neshama* (our soul). On Shabbat, we are granted more spiritual light and an expanded soul that has the capacity to take in that light. Just as physical light enables people to see more clearly to avoid tripping and falling, the spiritual light of Shabbat gives us more clarity to avoid the spiritual pitfalls and obstacles that often trip us up in our lives. Seeing clearly—physically and spiritually—is essential when trying to live in the present moment. Think of how, even in everyday language, people say, "Oh, I see!" when clarity comes to them. Being "in the dark" is a sure way to stumble and fall. Shabbat candles give us extra spiritual light to guide our way.

Candle lighting is done at the time when the sun's light is fading. Many cultures worship the sun as the intense, powerful, and essential source of light and heat that it is. The Jewish people, however, while grateful to God for creating the sun, turn their attention to the small flames of the Shabbat candles. While the physical world testifies to the power of the sun, Shabbat candles testify to the power of the spiritual and the unseen God as the source of all of Creation and all power. What a joyful reminder that the overwhelming power and presence of the physical world is just a garment cloaking the reality of the spiritual world that pervades everything. And that can be appreciated in the tiniest flame of a candle.

This simple reminder can help us reorient ourselves to the reality of the spiritual world, even when it appears that it is the physical world which has the stronger presence. Living in the present moment requires knowing that the spiritual dimension is the most real. We must respond to physical external circumstances and situations, but those have a bit of a façade attached to them. The small light of the Shabbat candles shifts us away from the strong power of the sun to the subtle power of the flame, reigniting the flame of our souls once again.

Now that we've connected with the spiritual light of Shabbat in this alcove, we'll move to the next alcove in our Shabbat Room.

WINE:
A FULL CUP OF JOY

Our eyes have now seen that it is Shabbat, and a sense of tranquility and relaxation has begun to both fill our souls and empty our minds of everything that distracts and distresses us. We're beginning to let go. The light of the Shabbat candles is still visible as we move to the next alcove. In this alcove, a filled-to-the-brim wine cup sits on a silver tray that catches the overflowing wine. The tray rests on an elegantly-covered table with a chair nestled by its side.

In most social gatherings, it would be improper to pour someone a glass of wine filled all the way to the top. But this is wine for Kiddush, the sanctification of Shabbat, and we want to see and drink from a cup that is overflowing. We want to understand fullness and completion not just as an idea but also as a real experience. Fullness and completion are underlying messages of Shabbat, and they are at the core of our state of mind when living in the present moment.

People often talk about the differences in people's attitudes toward life by describing them as "seeing the glass half empty" or "seeing the glass half full." On Shabbat, when we make Kiddush, the glass is not half full; it is completely full. All of us, but especially people with the "half empty" attitude toward life, have the opportunity with Kiddush to see and affirm that the glass is "full." Experiencing life as a "full cup" means more than being optimistic and positive—although those are also great qualities to possess.

WHO IS REALLY IN CONTROL?

We tend to be most convinced by what we see with our own eyes and experience for ourselves, and that becomes our reality. On Shabbat, we are allowed, in fact, we are commanded, to create and then step into sights, sounds, and tastes that define a specific reality: a reality that says everything is complete, whole, and finished—a reality that says that God is in control and, while we have been given important work to do in this world, we do not control the world. On Shabbat, we can stop pouring into the cup. The cup is full; our work is done.

People often drink wine to celebrate the completion of a big project or upon reaching a milestone. Our Kiddush wine is similar. Every week, we say we've reached the milestone of the week—Shabbat—and everything is complete. Not only is the cup full, but it is also filled with sweetness. Drinking wine is supposed to make us feel happy—the sweet, heady feeling that wine gives us at the physical level and the spiritual joy that comes from celebrating and toasting that we've arrived at our destination.

Shabbat is about stopping. Knowing when, why, and how to stop is key to celebrating Shabbat and in living life in the present moment. How, though, does Shabbat guide us in living every day in the present moment? If it's not Shabbat, what does "stopping" mean? The commandment to "rest" on Shabbat is preceded by the equal commandment to "work for six days." How do I know if it is a "work moment" or a "rest moment" during the six regular days of the week?

Interestingly, Shabbat has the potential to train us at the same time about work and rest and to become sensitive to the right combination of working and resting in any particular situation on any day of the week. The message of Shabbat pervades every day of the week. There is an element of completion in each step along the way.

This means that I can recognize that at any given moment, the glass is full. It may be a small glass, but it is filled nonetheless. When I see that even as I work, each stage of my action is what it is supposed to be for that moment, then my working (or pouring) can be done in a state of tranquility rather than anxiety. My work is done with energy and effort, but it has an element of rest within it. Just because something is in progress, doesn't mean that it's not complete for whatever point it has reached. Each step of a change stands alone as a point of completion.

We know many examples where we have accepted this as true; we simply need to apply it to more situations. For example, when a building is being built and blueprints are drawn, we appreciate the blueprints as complete for what they are; we don't bemoan the fact that the blueprints aren't the building. When a healthy baby is born, we are profoundly grateful that it's a baby. No one is expecting to give birth to a fully-grown, functioning adult.

WE ARE ALL WORKS IN PROGRESS ...

Even though everyone reading this is obviously no longer a newborn baby, we often overlook the reality that our entire life is a continuous unfolding of new stages and development. We are all works in progress and children growing and developing, and as the work continues and the child blossoms, each moment is complete. Each moment is a full cup.

When the cup is full, it's time to stop pouring and to start drinking. Deriving pleasure and drinking in the joy from our efforts and the blessings, with which we are so bountifully showered, is an obligation to both God and ourselves. Often we fail to appreciate the pleasure of the moment because we spend all our time, and give all our attention, to trying to fill the cup, failing to perceive the cup as full and believing instead it is forever in need of our never-ending pouring. The filled kiddush cup says, "Stop, sit down, and enjoy the fruit of the vine—the fruits of your life."

Living in the present moment means being able to recognize two important realities: at any moment, the cup is full and, at any moment, we can pause, relish the sweetness of our blessings, and drink a "*L'chaim* (to life)" with enjoyment.

As we leave this alcove, we notice the warm, sweet smell of challah bread that awaits us in the next alcove.

CHALLAH: ENJOYING TRUE WEALTH—THE GOLDEN LOAVES OF TRUST

The soft glow from the Shabbat candles has enveloped us, and a sense of relaxation from the sweet Kiddush wine is beginning to lift our spirits. Shabbat is becoming more than an abstract idea or interesting philosophy or theological concept; Shabbat is becoming an all-encompassing reality through each of our senses.

We follow the fragrance that wafts through the air ... and then we see them—two golden loaves of braided challah set out on a table for us. What a delicious aroma and a beautiful sight.

Interestingly, it is a custom to have the challah as the only food on the table when the blessing for it is made on Shabbat. This tradition symbolizes our desire to focus only on the bread, regardless of whatever else will be served afterward. Often, we fail to live in the present moment and enjoy it because we're always thinking about what's coming next instead of what is right in front of us. These small flights into the future can deprive us of pleasure that is here for us to experience now. On Shabbat, we have a dress rehearsal for living with an awareness of the present, and we have all the props we need to make it real.

You'll notice that there are two loaves of challah on the table. Even if you happen to be the only one at the meal, on Shabbat, we always put out two whole loaves of bread. The loaves can be small rolls; they just need to be whole. The two loaves symbolize the double portion of *manna*, the heavenly food the Jewish people survived on throughout their forty years in the Midbar (the wilderness). The gift of manna served to instill trust in God. The Jewish people were to internalize the idea that God is always providing for us and will always provide for us. Obviously, this lesson is not easy to learn. Otherwise, it wouldn't have required a daily experience for forty years. Every morning the amount of manna sufficient for one day's food would appear on the ground. People collected the manna and baked, cooked, or otherwise prepared it as they wanted. According to the Midrash, the manna tasted like anything a person desired. The only stipulation was that the manna could not be saved up, stored, or hoarded in any way. Anything that was left would rot—not because there was no refrigeration, but because God wanted to convey that the people's needs would be provided each day. We are supposed to understand this too, and know that each day's opportunities are for that day only.

When we procrastinate as a result of dwelling either in the past or the future, our manna is spoiling. Consider how many of us, from time to time, have some spoiled food (opportunities) in our dwelling places. Even though scientists have found ways to alter food to prolong shelf life, no one has yet discovered a way to do this with time.

A DOUBLE DOSE OF TRUST ...

Receiving the manna on a daily basis would seem sufficient training for someone to develop the trust that is necessary for living in the present moment. But there was a different arrangement on Shabbat. On Fridays, God would send a double portion of manna—enough to last for both Friday and Shabbat, and the Jewish people were forbidden from going out to gather manna on Shabbat. This is a real test and a real opportunity. On Shabbat, we are obligated to let go. On Shabbat, our souls long to let go. We must trust that God indeed gave us enough to last for two days, but it's oh-so-tempting to go out when it's right there and get a little bit more, "just in case."

Thus, the unique quality of Shabbat is paradoxical. I both indulge—no fasting allowed unless it is Yom Kippur (The Day of Atonement)—and I don't worry about not having enough. I know I have exactly what I need, and I can enjoy it without concern. That is true freedom and true happiness and the lesson of manna and of our double loaves of challah.

HAVDALAH: THE ABILITY TO DIFFERENTIATE

After enjoying the rest and true "re-creation" of our souls on Shabbat, we prepare to depart for our journey into the next week. We don't just turn and leave; there is as much ceremony given to taking leave of Shabbat as to entering it, and for that, we move to the fourth and final alcove of the Shabbat Room—Havdalah.

Havdalah, which literally means to differentiate or to distinguish, invites us to be aware of the difference between Shabbat and the rest of the week, between resting and working and all of the other differentiations that we must be able to make in life. The ability to distinguish between one thing and another is the basis of human intelligence and a prerequisite for spiritual growth. Havdalah gives us the opportunity to focus on paying attention to and developing that ability to differentiate. Just as the words taken from King Solomon's Kohelet (Ecclesiastes), and made famous in the song by The Byrds, tell us, "To everything there is a season, and a time for every purpose under heaven." Being able to live in the present moment requires, above all else, knowing the nature of the moment that is presenting itself to us. Expectations or perceptions that we are in one kind of situation, when we are in fact in another, will disorient and prevent us from truly experiencing what the moment has to offer or from knowing what we should do with that moment.

THE CHALLENGE OF TRANSITIONS ...

Frequently, transitions from one moment to another are not easy. As difficult as it can be to stop working and creating in order to enter into Shabbat, once we immerse ourselves in its restful holiness, it can be equally difficult to let go of it and gear up for another week of work. Even in general society, moving from the weekend to Monday morning is a challenge for many people. We don't hear of many "Thank God It's Monday" clubs. The ceremony of Havdalah, however, basically does say exactly this. Thank God we have work to do and a role in creating and perfecting the world.

The simple fact that there is a ceremony probably makes the most difference. Whether it is taking home party favors from a child's birthday party or a tote bag filled with goodies from a convention, it is easier to leave when we take something with us as a reminder of what we just experienced. That is exactly what the Havdalah ceremony is: we bring the wisdom of Shabbat, with all of its insight and inspiration, with us into the new week. Havdalah is our spiritual goody bag. How does it happen? Let's move into the Havdalah Alcove to see.

The first thing we notice is that the alcove looks similar to what we saw in the first two Shabbat alcoves. There is a candle and an overflowing cup of wine. There is something else on the table, too: a beautifully carved wooden spice box filled with cloves and cinnamon sticks.

THE SPIRITUAL NATURE OF WINE ...

Candles and wine were used to initiate Shabbat and they are used, in a slightly different way, to end Shabbat and transition to the regular week. The Havdalah ceremony reverses the order of the blessing on the candles and wine. With Shabbat, we began with the candles, and with Havdalah, we begin with the wine. Our sages have noticed that wine is always used in Jewish rituals when we desire to integrate the physical and the spiritual. One reason given is that most things in the physical world decay over time: food spoils, metals rust, wood decomposes, bodies weaken, and basically deterioration in one form or another sets in. Wine is an exception to this. When it is properly stored, time improves it and makes it more valuable. Cheap wines are new wines; expensive ones are vintage wines.

We associate this quality of improving over time with those things that are of a more spiritual nature, such as ancient wisdom and deep love, qualities that expand and become enhanced with time. So wine, being physical but with properties that relate to the spiritual, becomes the perfect vehicle to use for the sanctification of times and situations where we want to bring the physical and the spiritual together. Whether it is the sip of wine a baby has at his *brit milah* (circumcision) where the physical procedure he experiences is a symbol of the Divine covenant he is entering, the wine the bride and groom drink under the *chuppah* (marriage canopy) to symbolize the physical and spiritual union of their lives, or the wine we drink on Shabbat and the other festival holidays where we are keenly focused on creating a unified physical and spiritual experience, in each situation the wine is our down-to-earth reminder of the elevated reality we can create and in which we can live.

As the Sabbath ends, the challenges that our week is bound to bring will require keeping the message of wine with us. One of the significant challenges we will face is that many of the moments in which we will find ourselves will appear to be of a physical nature, having nothing to do with spirituality. With the ability to differentiate and the insight to see that every moment has the potential of wine—it can be both physical and spiritual—our weekday life can carry with it the taste of Shabbat wine.

SMELLING THE SWEET SPICES ...

After the blessing is made over the wine, we make a blessing over the spices, the fragrances of which we inhale deeply, as if we could hold onto it in every cell of our being. Our sense of smell is the one most directly and accurately linked to memory. We can walk into a house and smell something that reminds us, and takes us right back to, our childhood and a lifetime of smells: latkes frying on Chanukah or that unique combination smell of *matza*, *marror*, and *charoset* at the Passover Seder. Our sense of smell links us to our past, and when we smell the spices at Havdalah, we are taking in and holding onto the sweet memory of the Shabbat we have just experienced and bringing it into the week that is opening before us.

Whatever insights and wisdom we have gained from the spiritual rest of Shabbat, we need and want to take with us. Those memories have the ability to make our new week different. Whenever we are able to extract insight and wisdom from any situation in the past and bring it to the present, our lives will be enriched and sweetened. Of course, not all memories are pleasant ones; some are quite painful, and learning from past mistakes is bittersweet. A cinnamon stick, often used as a havdalah spice, is similar. It tastes quite bitter if you bite into it directly, but when you smell it or let it steep in a drink, it releases a fragrance and flavor that is enticing. Being able to sense our memories, even if we can't directly bite into them, can inspire and motivate us. We don't want to "let go" of our past. We want to learn from it, just as we bring the sweetness of Shabbat into our week and let its aroma spread and impart a holy fragrance to all that we do.

CARRYING A TORCH OF LIGHT INTO THE WEEK ...

Following the blessing made over the spices, we make a blessing over the candle. To begin Shabbat, we lit two separate candles. To end Shabbat, we bring a minimum of two flames together so that they are touching and create "a torch." Most people have the custom of lighting a special Havdalah candle made of three, six, or twelve strands. For Havdalah, we want an impressive flame to look at. The blessing for the candle also has a different emphasis and refers to the light of the fire (as opposed to the light of the Shabbat candles).

There is also a custom to turn off the lights when making Havdalah, which intensifies the impact of the light of the Havdalah flame. We think of using a torch when it is dark and we need to find our way. The Havdalah candle is the torch that symbolically lights our path during the week, when the spiritual dimension of life tends to darken and be less visible to us. This unique candle represents the spiritual light that we cling to throughout the week of distractions with which the ordinary physical world confronts us. The candle reminds us to pay attention to the spiritual opportunities that lie hidden within our mundane activities.

The Havdalah candle is a beacon of light that spans and joins our future vision with our decisions in the here and now—the essence of living in the present moment. This torch casts a light that illuminates the direction in which we want to proceed, while staying firmly planted in the choices we need to make right now. For example, someone who is holding the "torch" of medicine and wants to become a doctor in the future needs to take science classes in the present, do well in school, and make on-going choices consistent with the vision of becoming a doctor.

THE POWER TO IGNITE
OUR POTENTIAL ...

The fire of the candle also represents the power that we have to impact the world. Fire can be used both to destroy and to create. Our actions are always like fire—powerful and with the potential to affect the world, in either a beneficial or destructive way. Fire is never a neutral force and neither are we. Just as we are commanded to stop our creativity on Shabbat, we have an obligation to be creative the other six days of the week. On Shabbat, we express passive trust; we let go of our creative control of the world and trust that God is providing us with every-thing we need. As we start the workweek, we pick up our torch and move into a place of active trust, where we trust that God is lighting our way, providing us with whatever we need in order to do whatever we have to do. We have the opportunity and the obligation to move forward and contribute our efforts. God has created the fire and has put it into our hands to use. We move into the week with this question facing us: "How will I use this 'fire' that God has given me to move myself and the world forward this week?"

As we depart the Shabbat Room, the taste of Havdalah wine enlivens us, the fragrance of the spices energizes and inspires us, and the light of the fire guides us. With our power of distinction and differentiation heightened, we are ready to embrace the new week and all the moments that will come our way as we journey toward the next level of completion and the next Shabbat.

RHYTHM OF RENEWAL ...

The weekly rhythm of Shabbat guarantees that we never go more than six days without having the opportunity to renew and refresh our spiritual connection and reorient ourselves. Twenty-five hours of involving all our senses in living in the present moment makes us more accustomed to, and comfortable with, dwelling in the spiritual house of the present.

CONCLUDING BLESSING OF THE HAVDALAH CEREMONY ...

"Blessed are You, Hashem our God, Crowned Sovereign of the universe, who makes a distinction between holy and ordinary, between light and darkness, between Israel and the other nations, between the seventh day and the six working days. Praised are You, Hashem, who makes a distinction between holy and ordinary."

Shabbat is the most important and most frequent Jewish holiday. However, the Jewish calendar is richly laden with other holidays as well that invite us to tap into the spiritual wisdom and Divine energy that we need to help inspire us to live with awareness in the present moment. Let's move on to the next room in our House of the Present Moment, the Holiday Room.

III.

Holiday Room

INTRODUCTION

THE JEWISH YEAR IS FILLED WITH overlapping cycles—daily, weekly, monthly, and yearly—which, taken together, create a unique rhythm of life. We've left the Shabbat Room, where we learned about the weekly cycle that creates the foundation of Jewish life and that gives us the opportunity to re-center ourselves in the present moment. Now it's time to enter the room of Jewish holidays. In this room, we will find four of the many holidays that the Jewish people celebrate throughout the year, which enhance our awareness of different aspects of living in the present moment. Each holiday invites us to experience with all our senses what living in the present moment feels like, looks like, and even tastes like. While the underlying message of all the holidays is to live with trust in God in the present moment, each holiday has its own emphasis and its own story. If we immerse ourselves in the spiritual qualities of each holiday, we can enhance our ability to learn and grow from understanding and celebrating each one.

Like dining slowly and enjoying each part of a full-course meal, every holiday is a "course" to be savored, with its unique flavor to take in, physically and spiritually, for enjoyment, nourishment, and enlightenment. Living in the present moment requires being present physically, emotionally, and spiritually. Each of the holidays presents us with opportunities to do just that. Fortunately, the opportunities are not left undefined. We have the added benefit of each holiday coming with scripts, staging directions, and props to help us go beyond conceptualizing living in the present moment to actualizing it.

When we fully take in a holiday, it has the power to affect us continuously and long after the holiday is over. Just as physical nourishment from the food we eat becomes part of the very cells of our body, so too does the spiritual nourishment from the holidays become part of, and enhance, the essence of our spiritual abode, our spiritual home.

Although there are Jewish holidays in almost every month of the Jewish year, we've chosen four to feature in our Holiday Room, each in its own alcove: Rosh Chodesh, which is the celebration of the new moon and the new Jewish month; Rosh Hashanah and Yom Kippur; Sukkot; and Chanukah. The first alcove we will enter focuses on Rosh Chodesh, which is celebrated at least eleven times a year.

ROSH CHODESH: HOLDING ONTO THE LIGHT

As we come into the first alcove, it appears we have entered a completely dark place. Is there anything here? As our eyes become accustomed to the dark, however, we notice a tiny sliver of a moon and many stars in this otherwise unlit space. This is the Rosh Chodesh Alcove, where we can experience the monthly renewal of the moon and the beginning of the new Jewish month. It's a bit peculiar that there is a Jewish holiday that celebrates such a dark time. It certainly would be more interesting to celebrate the moon when it is a sleek and silvery half-moon—or when a plump orange harvest moon fills the night sky. That would get everyone's attention and would be much more exciting; instead, here we are, focusing on the darkest day of the month when the moon is barely visible. Rosh Chodesh, the beginning of the new month, is unlike any of the other holidays. Rosh Chodesh is celebrated eleven or twelve times during the year (twelve during a leap year). It must be important and have something special to teach us.

Being patient and not losing trust in dark times ...

One dimension of Rosh Chodesh is related to the darkness that surrounds the holiday itself. We always associate darkness with difficulty and pain. These don't really seem to be feelings or situations that we'd want to celebrate. However, it is specifically times of difficulty and pain that test us, when we are likely to find opportunities for spiritual growth. Does the darkness make us afraid? Do we lose hope? Or do we trust that the moon will be full once again? Do we realize that goodness is the ultimate purpose of Creation and that all things are moving in that direction, even when it doesn't appear that way and it is very dark? The Jewish people are compared to the moon that waxes and wanes. Each of our individual lives is a microcosm of the moon as well. We are all going through a process of becoming, and we are supposed to trust the process because we trust the ultimate result. The Jewish people have been given the holiday of Rosh Chodesh as a nation, and as individuals, to celebrate and cultivate trust in God. Being able to look in the sky over a period of a month and watch the moon go from darkness, to a sliver, to a half, and then to a full moon lets us witness with our own eyes a physical model of how life flows. We can practice trusting that dark and difficult times are part of Creation. We are not meant merely to endure them but rather to utilize them to develop qualities like courage, patience, and compassion that are essential during times of darkness, stress, and pain.

ROSH CHODESH AS ROSH CHADASH ...

After being in Miriam's Courtyard and finding out how we can read Hebrew words in different ways, you won't be too surprised to learn that the words Rosh Chodesh, which mean "beginning of the month," can also be read in another way. The words can be read as *Rosh Chadash*, which means "a new head." Does this mean we get a new head at least eleven times a year? The truth is that we have that opportunity open to us. Eleven times a year, we have a chance to renew ourselves, just as the moon's cycle is renewed. We can clear and refocus our minds and move in new directions. Physically, the direction our head is facing determines the direction we will go. Similarly, our mindset—where our heads are focused—impacts the direction and the course our lives will then take.

The day before every Rosh Chodesh is considered a mini-Yom Kippur or a small Day of Atonement. This mini-Yom Kippur gives us the opportunity to make changes and receive forgiveness for our mistakes, so that we can begin the new month with a fresh start. Most of us think of this chance coming just once a year in the fall when we observe Rosh Hashanah and Yom Kippur. Since it is human nature to get stuck in our perceptions, thoughts, and behaviors, repeating our errors and reliving the past, Rosh Chodesh can shake us out of our complacency and old habits. Rosh Chodesh reminds us that eleven times a year, God creates a new opportunity for us, giving us the gift of a clear head, a clean start, and a changed direction. In order to benefit from this opportunity, we need to know that it's there and then take advantage of the potential.

CHARTING A NEW COURSE
EACH MONTH ...

Since most of us function primarily in the general culture and orient our lives to the secular calendar, it is challenging to focus on Rosh Chodesh. While the most frequently occurring holiday, Rosh Chodesh is usually the most overlooked. If Rosh Chodesh would only coincide with the turning of the calendar page, maybe we'd pay more attention to it. But since the Jewish calendar is primarily lunar, there's almost never a match. There is nothing wrong with taking stock of ourselves, letting go of past mistakes, charting a new course on January first (or the beginning of any secular month or following Monday). However, we have a different opportunity on Rosh Chodesh, because the astronomical cycle of the moon is pulling, just as it does the tides of the oceans, in the direction of renewal. Being part of this cosmic experience brings us an intensified flow of energy that helps us change and enables us to tap into the incredible potential that this new month has for us. It is as if we can ride the wave that will bring us more quickly to shore. One of the psalms recited on Rosh Chodesh says, "This is the day that God has made; let us rejoice and be glad on it." (Psalm 118) This day of Rosh Chodesh and this moment in time—not yesterday and not tomorrow—is our gift. If during the month, we find ourselves slipping out of the present moment, and if fear has dragged us off course and into the pitfalls of living in the past or the future, Rosh Chodesh comes to catch us and return us to the present moment once again.

To everything there is a season and a time for every purpose under heaven …

We now return to those verses from Ecclesiastes that were popularized in a song written by Pete Seeger and sung by The Byrds. "To everything there is a season, and a time for every purpose under heaven." (Ecclesiastes 3:1–8). The words and even the cadence of the poetry are part of the message of Rosh Chodesh.

> *"A time to be born and a time to die,*
> *A time to plant and a time to uproot the planted,*
> *A time to weep and a time to laugh,*
> *A time to seek and a time to lose,*
> *A time to be silent and a time to speak."*
> *The Wisdom of King Solomon – Ecclesiastes*

Every Jewish month has a uniquely positive and powerfully spiritual energy associated with it that relates to the Jewish holiday that will occur during that month. The spiritual energy is not limited to the day or days of the holiday alone, but rather pervades the entire month. It is a propelling force.

We know that during any given week, each day has its own feeling. Most people feel very differently on Mondays than they do on Fridays. While this is usually related to the routine of our work, school, and activity schedules, time is not a flat, neutral backdrop against which our lives unfold. God has created time with certain spiritual qualities and energy frequencies that create a texture and depth. When we're aware of them, we will enter a flow that makes our journey through time more interesting and meaningful.

ALIGNING OURSELVES WITH THE
ENERGY OF EACH MONTH ...

For example, the month of Adar, which includes the holiday
of Purim and comes in the month of February or March, is designated as a time for an increased amount of joy. Someone who un-
derstands that can focus their attention and efforts on recognizing
and creating joy in their life and in the lives of others. Knowing
that their choices are being made in, and even impacted by, a time
that is auspicious for these particular attempts at creating joyful-
ness, changes the focus of their attitudes and actions. And while
every day in the month of Adar may not feel happy, due to an individual's personal circumstances, we need to know that joy is the
underlying mood and energy pulsating throughout each day of the
month and can lift everyone up along the way. We have access to
a higher dimension of joy at this time, so it makes sense to put our
efforts into actions that are moving in the same direction of the
flow of life. Cultivating an awareness of the spiritual qualities and
energies of each month is an essential step in taking full advantage
of the opportunities that each month's energy gifts us.

We need to ask ourselves, "Is this month about joy, or redemption, or dedication, or change, or new growth?" When we
recognize each of these uniquely different months and align ourselves with them, we will be able to live more purposefully in the
moment that is presented to us. (See the Glossary for the specific
themes of each Hebrew month.) Again, one could choose to focus on joy, redemption, dedication, change, or new growth at any
time of the year. Why not do it, though, at the time when the
Creator has designated a specific month, with its dedicated and
unique energy that channels all the forces, physical and spiritual,

to support and accelerate our spiritual growth? Every moment has momentum in it. With each Rosh Chodesh, our challenge is to seize the moment and the unique opportunity offered, riding the wave of a new flow of energy that is coming our way. The energy of Rosh Chodesh is powering and empowering everything throughout Creation—including us.

There is one time during the year where the new month is not celebrated as a new month, but rather as the beginning of a new year. Rosh Hashanah, the "head of the year," occurs on Rosh Chodesh Tishrei, but the fact that an entirely new year is being launched supersedes our focus on Rosh Chodesh, the beginning of an individual month. The next alcove we will visit will help awaken us to the spiritual potential of our first holiday of the new year—Rosh Hashanah—as well as its companion, Yom Kippur (The Day of Atonement), which follows ten days later.

ROSH HASHANAH AND YOM KIPPUR: WAKING UP TO GREATNESS

All of the alcoves we've visited so far have had something to see in them. The Rosh Hashanah and Yom Kippur Alcove is different. In addition to sight, we also experience sound—the rich, deep tones of the *shofar*, the ram's horn blown on the High Holidays. As we enter the alcove, we see walls that are awash with vibrant hues of sunrise, letting us know that we are in a place where we can experience the feeling of the dawn of a new day and a new year. To help enter a state of contemplation, we can sit in the white-cushioned chairs that line the alcove and we can think. Lest we become too relaxed, though, the awe-inspiring sounds of the shofar echoing in the background call us with a sense of urgency and rouse us from the lull of complacency that our daily routines often create. The time to wake up and embrace the opportunity to repair, return, and reunite our physical self with our eternal soul is right now.

The shofar, which we often associate only with the days of Rosh Hashanah and Yom Kippur, is actually blown every morning for thirty days prior to Rosh Hashanah (except Shabbat). Beginning with the first day of the Hebrew month of Elul, the shofar blasts call out to us to wake up to the present moment and the path of transformation that has been widened for us at this season. Although teshuvah—returning to our true spiritual selves—is always possible, the High Holidays provide specific moments in time that have the energy of teshuvah pulsing through them.

Rosh Hashanah and Yom Kippur are called the High Holidays because they do, in fact, take us to a "high" place, as they elevate us above our ordinary perspectives and have the potential to transport us to a higher level of being. While Rosh Hashanah and Yom Kippur are each holidays in their own right, the two holidays are woven together along with the entire month of Elul, which precedes the High Holiday season. Taken together, we are offered a forty-day plan and path of spiritual awakening and change.

CATCHING THE WAVE OF TESHUVAH (SPIRITUAL RETURN) ...

This is an auspicious time because it is a designated time. Like a surfer who catches the perfect wave, making the trip to shore faster and easier, when we catch the wave of any holiday, we ride on the spiritual energy of that specific holiday and reach our destination with greater ease and speed. Because waking up and pulling ourselves out of our habits and ruts is so challenging, whether we are stuck in the pain of past errors or in the fear of the future, taking advantage of this time of teshuvah makes that whole process much easier.

The order of the two holidays tells us a lot about living in the present moment and what it requires. We might think that Yom Kippur, the Day of Atonement on which we acknowledge our mistakes, should come before Rosh Hashanah, the New Year.

Shouldn't we have to take care of last year's issues before beginning a new year? Rosh Hashanah seems like it should be the "reward" for going through Yom Kippur. Surprisingly, Rosh Hashanah comes first. And even before it comes, we are given a daily "wake-up call," with the shofar blasts for the entire month of Elul. Rosh Hashanah has to come first because until we awaken to the reality that change is possible, a new year would just be the old year revisited. Until we know fully that a new year is being given to us to recreate our lives, we will continue to reenact what we've done in previous years that got us stuck or off track in the first place.

Once we are alert and present to the moment we are being given, and all the exciting potential it holds, we can then go through the detailed teshuvah process that culminates with Yom Kippur. Yom Kippur is the cleansing process that helps us bring what we need from the past and the future to our new place in the present. We need to bring both the wisdom gained from our mistakes of the past and the vision of our future that guides us to our new year—our new dwelling place in the present that God has given us at Rosh Hashanah.

"LET US MAKE MAN ..."

It should be a source of consolation and comfort to us to know that it is human nature to forget that God brought us into the world to grow and develop. Thankfully, our physical growth happens almost automatically; we don't need to set the alarm to remind a child to grow an inch this coming year. Our spiritual selves, however, require much more active involvement. Rosh Hashanah, which commemorates and celebrates the creation of Adam, hints at this. Before God creates the first human being, He says, "Let us create Man." There are many commentators who ask, "Who is us if God is One?" One response is that God is speaking to the human being himself and letting him know that his creation is going to be a joint project between God and man. We have to invest ourselves in our own creation. Rosh Hashanah reminds us that while our bodies may practically function on autopilot, our souls cannot. We have to stay alert and get involved.

Even at this time of teshuvah, when the process of transformation is easier, there is still a lengthy process required. The shofar is blown for thirty days in a row in the synagogue during the morning service. These days, combined with the ten days that join Rosh Hashanah and Yom Kippur, which culminates with yet another shofar blast, bring us to a total of forty days. It takes forty days of concentrated effort to wake up, stay alert, and focus on the new beginning and the possibilities for profound change that are accessible to us.

TRANSFORMATION AND THE POWER OF 40 ECHO ONCE AGAIN ...

As we discovered earlier, we associate the number forty with the process of transformation. Not only is it significant in events in the Torah, for the Jewish people as a nation, and for a human pregnancy, but the number forty echoes throughout Jewish life and living as a recurring theme. Here, we see it in the context of the process of teshuvah—our own ongoing process of personal growth and rebirth.

Each of these examples reminds us to be patient and persistent with our own process of transformation. Needing a shofar blast to wake us up is fine. Just as a person who is willing to set the alarm clock and be jolted by its shocking blast is the one who gets up and gets moving, so too a person needs to hear the shofar blast to wake up and get motivated and energized to pursue spiritual growth. Waking up and getting out of our familiar and comfortable habits and not hitting the "snooze button" of life is a considerable accomplishment. Long after Rosh Hashanah and Yom Kippur have ended, we have the opportunity and ability to hear the shofar's call in our mind. Each time we do this, we realize that the High Holidays are meant to awaken us to the real "high" of life: transformation is possible at every moment we're willing to engage in the step-by-step process of working on returning to and reconnecting with our most authentic and true spiritual selves.

Coming out of Rosh Hashanah and Yom Kippur in a more awakened state of being, enables us to take a new look at how we can move forward and live our everyday lives with all their challenges. Our next alcove is devoted to this idea with the holiday of Sukkot—the holiday that calls us out of our permanent homes with their illusion of physical safety and into our temporary *sukkah*, with its comfort of spiritual security.

SUKKOT: FINDING SECURITY IN A TEMPORARY WORLD

Something feels very different in the next alcove of the Holiday Room. This alcove is dedicated to Sukkot. Sukkot is a wonderful holiday celebrated in the fall. One of its central observances is to build and spend time in a temporary "booth" called a *sukkah*. Being in a sukkah feels almost childlike—somewhat like being in a tree house, but on the ground. In order to enter this alcove, we move through French doors and onto an outdoor patio. Here, we experience the surprise and pleasure of finding an actual sukkah, with its wood-slatted roof open to the sky and dappled sunlight peeking through the pine boughs that loosely cover the slats. A table and two chairs await us so we can sit in the sukkah and bask in the unique experience of being in both the sun and the shade, inside and outside, sheltered and exposed. If you go into the Sukkot alcove on a clear night, you'll see the stars and perhaps the moon.

The sukkah isn't always a comfortable place to be. On some days it is cold and windy; it might be raining or snowing, and on occasion, the whole roof might fall and the sukkah might need to be built all over again.

TRUST IN GOD'S SPIRITUAL
PROTECTION ...

Sukkot is the holiday that commemorates the visible Divine protection that the Jewish people lived with during the forty years in the Midbar (the wilderness). The Torah teaches us that we are to observe the holiday of Sukkot because "God caused the Jewish people to dwell in sukkot." (Leviticus 23:43). We don't know whether the sukkot that the Torah refers to as the Jews' dwelling places were actual structures, such as the ones we build and dwell in during the seven-day festival of Sukkot, or whether they refer to the Clouds of Glory. These divine Clouds, with which God sheltered the people during their wanderings, protected them from heat and cold. In either case, the sukkah we build allows us to live for one week of the year with a clearer sense that God is the source of our protection and security.

When we dwell in the sukkah—eating, sleeping, and spending time—we have an opportunity to demonstrate our trust in God's protection. Interestingly, the mitzvah is not to just go outdoors and be completely exposed to the elements and nature, but rather to actively build a sukkah that does provide some sort of protection, albeit fragile. Why is this?

The sukkah, which must have a roof of natural materials and be partially open to the sky and exposed to the elements, reinforces the truth that nothing we can construct in the physical world can provide complete safety. Security only exists in the spiritual realm and comes from God alone. The sukkah reminds us that the physical world is fragile, despite all our efforts to make ourselves "safe." Ultimately, not only are physical things such as houses, buildings, cars, and possessions fragile, but so are our circumstances. Jobs, health, financial situations, physical abilities, and much more can change in an instant.

SPIRITUAL SECURITY VS. PHYSICAL SAFETY ...

What is the attitude we're trying to cultivate toward the physical world that we clearly inhabit? The sukkah tells us to be involved in the physical world. Build your "sukkah": build your homes, buy life insurance, and join an exercise class, but don't rely on these things to provide you with ultimate protection and safety. When we put our trust in things and in circumstances, as we are tempted to do by our nature and by our cultural conditioning, we are stepping into a world of illusion. We desperately want to believe that we can have protection in the physical world through our bank accounts, security systems, and exercise programs. The sukkah, with its required temporariness and fragility, conveys and presents us with a more truthful picture of reality. Sitting in the sukkah invites a challenge to our illusion of the strength and seeming permanence of the physical things that we invest in to make us feel safe.

Even if our sukkah does occasionally collapse, its message tells us that we can forge ahead and rebuild without the anger, angst, and anxiety that usually accompany situations when what we have relied on falls apart. Our sukkah represents the reality of the world, as it reminds us that everything in the physical world is temporary. Things break, wear out, deteriorate, get old, and crumble. Only that which exists in the spiritual world is eternal and unlimited and truly strong and secure. Recognizing this reality about the physical world leads us to an important question. What are we, spiritual beings, doing in a physical world and how are we supposed to relate to it? Fortunately, we have an answer. The true purpose of the physical world is as a means and vehicle to help us create spiritual connections and reach our spiritual potential. It is only with the realization of the role that the physical world plays in our life that we can have the balance and perspective that enable us to live with spiritual joy in a fragile physical world.

Building a sukkah and, more importantly, a sukkah mentality for the entire year creates joy and happiness. Perhaps this is one reason Sukkot is called *Z'man Simchateinu*, the "Holiday of Our Joy." Deep joy comes from truly knowing what is real in this world and what we can trust and knowing what is an illusion and fragile. We can leave worry and fear, which kick us out of the present moment, at the door of the sukkah as we enter the place and space that speak to us about trust, security, and what is real. The sukkah is said to encompass the Shechinah, the Divine Presence. Letting the Divine Presence engulf us is the source of our security in this world and allows us to dwell serenely in the present moment.

We take leave of the Sukkot alcove to move into the next alcove, which focuses on Chanukah. It appears to be dark, like the Rosh Chodesh alcove that we've already visited.

CHANUKAH: BREAKING THROUGH THE VEIL OF LIMITATIONS

The alcove we are now entering is darkened because Chanukah, the next holiday we will experience, occurs at the darkest time of the year and at the darkest time of the month. However, the alcove is not completely dark because we are pulled in by the soft glow of a large silver Chanukah menorah with eight brightly dancing flames (plus the one shamash). Chanukah commemorates two miracles: the military victory and the miracle of the oil. The Maccabees (though few in number) defeated the army of the Syrian Greeks who wanted to destroy Judaism. Miraculously, the small flask of oil needed to kindle the Menorah for the rededication of the Temple in Jerusalem lasted for eight days. That was the second miracle. Chanukah teaches us about being in a situation and facing overwhelming odds with the apparent reality of limited resources to overcome those odds. Whether it was the small, rag-tag military group that prevailed over the Syrian Greek military machine or the small flask of oil that lasted for the eight days of dedication, the Chanukah story inspires us to look at our own challenging situations differently.

We often face difficult situations that threaten to overwhelm us. We feel unprepared and ill-equipped to deal with the obstacles and apparent limitations in the resources and resolve need-ed to address them. Chanukah teaches us that we, like the Mac-cabees, can step forward and trust that whatever God has given us is enough to start the process of facing and overcoming our challenges. Going forward with this trust can trigger a miracle which enables us to achieve victory. The interesting thing about the miracle that can occur is that it usually has a relationship with the very resource we thought was limited. We define a miracle as something which happens which we don't expect because of our perceptions of natural limitations. A small amount of oil, burning at a "normal" rate, doesn't last for eight days. The miracle of the oil cruse in the Temple was that the oil ended up being enough for the eight-day dedication ceremony. The natural limitations were removed.

TRANSCENDING OUR PRECONCEIVED PERCEPTIONS ...

Why does trust have this impact? Is it magic? Not really. What trust says is this: "I trust that God is the source of everything, including nature and natural laws." Being the source of nature, God has the power also to intervene in nature, and does. We may be bound to nature and the natural course of things because we have ascribed total power to it—in a way worshipping nature—and have forgotten who the real source of power in the cosmos is. When we transcend our preconceived perceptions through trust and recognize the power behind nature, the limitations of the physical world, which are ordinarily in effect, can melt away. It is as if a veil gets removed. There are actually two realities at any given situation in any moment: the physical reality where we experience natural limitations, and the spiritual reality which often offers the opportunity to transcend perceived limitations. Transcendence requires more than professing a belief: action is what triggers miracles.

A famous story about the prophet Elisha, who goes to help a righteous but impoverished widow, shows us how to put our beliefs into action. (II Kings 4:1-7) The widow's financial situation is dire and the only resource she has is one pitcher of oil. Elisha tells her to collect a large number of jars and to close the door of her home. She is to pour the oil from her one pitcher into each of the larger pitchers she has gathered. Because the poor woman trusts God, miraculously, her one pitcher of oil is able to fill all of the other pitchers. She then sells these at the market and is able to generate enough money to feed and clothe her family. Significantly, she doesn't find wealth from a rich uncle leaving her a large inheritance, discover a treasure buried in her backyard, or win the lottery. The miracle takes place with the very thing she initially thought was limited—her oil.

Just start ...

The challenge is to start with what we have, even if it's not "enough," and where it might not be natural, rational, or seem realistic to expect success. This active trust has the ability to transform reality. Chanukah is about transcending natural and normal limitations through actions, rooted in trust. The eight days of Chanukah, commemorated by the eight lights, remind us of what eight symbolizes—transcendence of nature and natural limitations. (The brit milah—circumcision—which takes place on the eighth day after birth also alludes to transcendence because it is a reminder that the individual can transcend his natural animal nature and develop his unlimited spiritual potential.) The Chanukah menorah is a visual and experiential reminder of the miracles that await us when we encounter our small cruse of oil, see through nature's veil of limitations, recognize God as the source of everything, and move forward in trust.

All the challenges we face in our lives have something in common. We can live the lessons of Chanukah and embrace the menorah as a beacon of light and our eternal symbol of how to move forward with trust. We can take actions that can trigger miracles—large and small—as we journey through the ups and downs of living.

We have explored each alcove in the Holiday room and have been inspired by the fact that the holidays which occur only once a year have meaning and lessons for us to use at any time throughout the year. We aren't limited to accessing the wisdom of the holidays only when they occur. What we've experienced and learned in each alcove can help us expand our understanding of what each holiday has to offer us every day of our lives as we continue our journey of learning to live in the present moment.

Although we are leaving the Holiday Room, the next room we are going to move into also features a holiday. Passover, the most widely celebrated holiday of the year, is similar to Shabbat in that it is central to Jewish life. Passover commemorates the exodus from Egypt and marks the Creation of the Jewish people as a nation. Although Passover, like the other holidays, only occurs once a year, we are commanded to remember our exile and redemption from Egypt every single day of our lives. So now, we'll move into the Passover Room to explore the depth of what it has to teach us.

IV.

Passover Room

INTRODUCTION

PASSOVER IS THE HOLIDAY on the Jewish calendar that forms the foundation of Jewish life. It was the dramatic, pivotal moment when the Jewish people became a nation with the mission to serve God. It is also the holiday that gives us the opportunity to create the spiritual foundation of our House of the Present. When we spoke about the materials for building our house, we focused on using our memories, imagination, and power of choice. The holiday of Passover is a week-long immersion in using our memories to retrieve wisdom, our imagination to create a vision, and our power of choice to live in a completely transformed way—all without leaving the comfort of our physical homes.

As we enter the Passover Room, we see a familiar-looking *seder* plate on a table, holding all the ceremonial foods: *maror* (bitter herbs), *charoset* (chopped apples, nuts, and wine), a shank bone, and a hardboiled egg. Next to the *seder* plate is a plate of *matza*, four cups of wine, and a larger, fifth cup of wine nearby. Each of the alcoves in the Passover Room will give us a closer look at, and taste of, some of the ceremonial foods and traditions that we use not only in celebrating our Passover *seder*, but also to use as tools for learning to live in the present moment.

What this Passover Room will reveal to us is that it doesn't have to be Passover to access the rich insights that the holiday teaches us. Passover is a holiday with detailed ritual and order. In fact, the word *seder* means order, and gives us a hint that we have the ability to create seder (order) in our thoughts, speech, and actions whenever we desire. We don't need to wait until Passover comes. We can bring Passover with us into any moment throughout the year. Our seder, our order, has more to do with ordering our priorities than with sequencing events or tasks. If we have made unhealthy choices about how to use our time, pondering in which sequence or order we should do things is irrelevant. The priority of living with trust in the present moment, and of building a life with that focus, can be done using the rituals of our Passover seder. We will explore that in each of the alcoves. The first alcove features *matza*, a simple food with a profound message.

MATZA:
THE SIMPLE BREAD OF LIFE

Matza is probably the most universally recognized symbol and food for Passover, and as we enter the first Passover alcove, a simple stack of matza on a ceramic platter awaits us on the table. It is difficult to imagine what important message matza has to teach us. Yet this bread, made simply with flour and water, has the potential to help us focus on some of the most significant aspects of the present moment with each dry and crumbly bite. Perhaps it is because we are not distracted by a melt-in-your-mouth, palate-pleasing physical experience when we eat matza that we are able to "taste" the spiritual flavor of matza and heighten our awareness.

IT ISN'T EASY TO BE SIMPLE ...

Matza represents the joining of Heaven and Earth, the spiritual and the physical. Matza is made with flour and water—wheat from the ground and water from the heavens. Achieving simplicity is a basic tenet of living in the present moment, though it should not be confused with being easy or naïve. When we speak of simplicity, we are concerned with removing what is extraneous and irrelevant and clarifying that which is essential and important. It isn't easy being simple. Eating matza reminds us that simplification is possible and that we can cultivate a matza mentality all year round. Perhaps keeping a box of matza within reach in our kitchens to munch on throughout the year at moments when simplicity seems out of reach could help us "taste" the clarity we aspire to maintain.

Matza also has very specific requirements for preparation. Once the water and flour come together, the dough maker must mix, roll out, and bake the dough within eighteen minutes. Most of us are familiar with the significance of the number eighteen being the *gematria* (numerical equivalent) of the word "*chai,*" which means life. Matza is "life bread" that has a sense of urgency in its very creation. If the eighteen minutes are exceeded, the dough is considered "*chametz,*" which literally means "soured or spoiled" and we can't eat it during Passover. Why do we make such a fuss about how long it takes to prepare the matza? There's so little to matza, why is it ruined if we take a little bit longer to make it?

TIME IS OF THE ESSENCE ...

Matza as "life bread" is telling us something very important about our lives and about how we need to be fully engaged in the present moment. Life brings us a flow of wonderful opportunities for spiritual growth, disguised as "things to do." These opportunities come with expiration dates. The baking of matza predated Benjamin Franklin's saying of "Don't put off 'til tomorrow what you can do today" by more than 3,000 years. We don't always perceive that there is or will be a difference between putting something off until later compared with doing it right now. However, the strict time deadline for the preparation of matza tells us that there is a difference. We need to be fully focused on what choices and opportunities are in front of us at the moment, so we don't let them sour and become chametz.

BREAD OF AFFLICTION AND BREAD OF REDEMPTION ...

One of the names of Passover is "*Chag haMatzot*," which means the Festival of Matza. This clearly tells us that matza carries a central message of the holiday. We refer to matza as the "Bread of Affliction," as well as the "Bread of Redemption." The Exodus from Egypt is the event which transformed the Jewish people from enslavement with all of its afflictions, to redemption, which freed the Jewish people to serve the Creator of the universe. When we eat matza, we internalize the past with its afflictions and the future with its redemption in the same bite. As the bread of affliction, matza represents the physical oppression and deprivations that the Egyptians inflicted upon us. It is definitely the pain of the past. As the bread of redemption, though, matza also represents the basic, simple clarity that true spiritual freedom brings.

When we taste the matza as the bread of affliction, demonstrating that this was all we had, we are called upon to remember our suffering and pain and extract wisdom from that experience. It is a commandment of the Torah to remember both our slavery in, and our exodus from, Egypt. From that suffering, we should develop a soft heart and a passion for relieving the suffering of other people. In this case, "no pain, no gain" refers to our spiritual well-being, rather than our physical health.

Extracting matza (wisdom)
out of mitzrayim (pain)

מַצָּה Matza
מִצְרִים Mitzrayim

If nothing more, we can extract the wisdom to cultivate sensitivity and empathy for others from all the painful moments of our lives. A further hint that we are supposed to take something with us from our experience in Egypt comes from the Hebrew spelling of matza. Matza is spelled *Mem-Tzadi-Heh*. The first two letters ("*Mem*" and "*Tzadi*") are the same as the first two letters of the Hebrew word for Egypt, which is Mitzrayim and is spelled "*Mem-Tzadi-Reish-Yud-Mem*." We see that there is always the potential to extract a little bit of matza from Mitzrayim, a bit of wisdom from our pain.

Matza vs. chametz:
sensitivity vs. sourness

מַצָּה Matza (Sensitivity)
חמץ Chametz (Sourness)

As we've said, it is forbidden to eat chametz (sour) or leavened products on Passover. Interestingly, chametz is also spelled with a "*Mem*" and a "*Tzadi*" (*Chet-Mem-Tzadi*). Perhaps we are being told that when we leave Mitzrayim (Egypt), we must choose to take the *Mem* and *Tzadi* with us in the form of matza—and the sensitivity, compassion, and wisdom that it symbolizes—rather than leave Mitzrayim with the *Mem* and *Tzadi* in the form of chametz and the sourness, bitterness, and resentment that it symbolizes. We don't want to become people who are soured on life because of the challenges we've encountered and endured.

SIMPLE SUSTENANCE ...

When we are spiritually focused, the simple sustenance of matza can satisfy us. This is a form of freedom. We are redeeming ourselves from being enslaved by an endless quest for physical gratification. We are fine as long as we have basic sustenance. We probably all know people who seem to require a never-ending stream of novel, exciting, "tasty" experiences in order to feel satisfied. They are living a life of enslavement chained to their physical desires and are never "free" to enjoy the simple things in their lives. Satisfaction is a spiritual state of being and a personal choice we each can make. It is liberating to feel nourished by and satisfied with the simplicity of matza.

Matza, then, becomes a symbol of our origin (enslavement), our path (liberation), and our destination (freedom). The simple ingredients of matza, the limited window of time for its preparation, its taste, and even its spelling, all help us gain a better understanding of the present moment. We have a chance, in essence, to taste the present moment—being on the cusp of change that requires a firm grasp of the wisdom extracted from a painful past and of the vision of a redeemed future—with each crispy bite.

While they were still in Egypt, the Jewish people received a command to eat the Passover offering with matza and *maror* (bitter herbs) to celebrate their fast-approaching exodus from Egyp-

tian bondage. We can easily understand how matza is meaningful for this ceremony, but why would the command tell them to
dwell on their bitter enslavement through the eating of maror, if
they were about to become free? In our next alcove, we'll come to
understand and appreciate the role of maror, bitter herbs, in the
Passover seder and their symbolic meaning for us in our process
of learning to live in the present moment.

MAROR: JUST BECAUSE IT'S BITTER, DOESN'T MEAN IT'S BAD

The second alcove in this Room has a small table with two plates—one holds the bitter herbs (maror) and one contains the sweet *charoset*, made with chopped apples and nuts that are sweetened with wine and cinnamon. Let's learn how this bitter and sweet combination teaches us about living in the present.

THE MAROR CHALLENGE ...

There is the moment at the Passover seder that everyone slightly dreads: eating the maror, the bitter herbs. However, there is also a small feeling of pride and accomplishment when it is eaten, and sometimes even some competition about who was able to eat the biggest piece—especially if horseradish root is used for the maror.

PAIN IS INEVITABLE; SUFFERING IS OPTIONAL ...

Our approach to eating maror is a good metaphor for living our lives in the present moment. Often, we try to escape what is happening in the moment because we fear pain. While we certainly don't want to go looking for pain and bitterness in our lives, the truth is that everyday living brings a certain amount of maror (pain) with it. It's fine to feel a slight sense of dread, but we will go further in life if we cultivate a sense of pride and accomplishment when we encounter a bitter moment, succeed in dealing with it, and learn from it. We can view our life as a seder plate, knowing that there will always be some maror on it. Although pain in life is inevitable, suffering is optional. Suffering is a prolonged sense of being surprised, upset, and angry that one is experiencing pain. It diverts our attention and energy from growing from our challenges. It keeps us immobilized. But we always have the power to seek a sense of accomplishment over a sense of suffering

The Torah commands us to eat the Passover sacrifice on matza with bitter herbs. "They shall eat the flesh on that night—roasted over the fire—and matzot; with bitter herbs shall they eat it." (Exodus 12:8). It appears that one of the prerequisites of the Exodus from Egypt, the redemption from Mitzrayim (enslavement), is the ability to eat the bitter herbs. Our eating of the bitter herbs hints at another aspect of pain. The bitter herbs are, after all, still food. The commandment does not say to swallow sharp objects or a non-food item that causes pain. We are eating food that is bitter, but it *is* food nonetheless, and it has the power to nourish us in its own way. Painful and bitter times can give us opportunities for growth that may not come in any other way. Just as our goal isn't to avoid going to a seder because we don't want to eat maror, our goal in life isn't to avoid living in the present moment because it might bring some pain our way.

BENEFITING FROM BITTERNESS ...

We remember that Miriam's name means "bitter waters" and was an acknowledgment of the bitter situation that the Jewish people faced in Egypt. Of course, Miriam recognized the bitterness of her situation, but she didn't allow it to be the determining characterization of her reality. Maror wasn't the only food on her plate. Because of this, she was able to lift up the people spiritually. She read her name not only as Miriam (bitter waters) but also as Mayrim (to lift up). We can do the same thing when we acknowledge that we have maror on our plate—bitterness in our lives—which may be difficult to swallow and digest, but that we must eat. Like the nourishment the maror gives us, the lessons we learn from bitter experiences can also give us energy, lifting us up and propelling us forward in our lives.

PAIN WITH PURPOSE ...

All of our past experiences, whether painful or pleasurable, have the potential to change our perspective about life and make us wiser. It is a Jewish tradition that a person is supposed to stand up when an elderly person enters the room, even if the elderly person isn't particularly accomplished in any way. We consider the wisdom of experience that a person gathers just from living his or her life over a number of decades entitles him or her to this honor. We cannot age completely unscathed by life's trials and tribulations. But we do have the unique challenge, which is a gift from God, of trying to extract the wisdom that lies in each bitter bite we have to swallow along the way. If the Jewish people had left

Mitzrayim glad only to get away from the slavery and oppression, without having learned anything from the 210 years they spent there, their painful experience would have been purposeless. Pain without purpose causes even more suffering. We know that the pain of enslavement in Mitzrayim benefited the Jewish people because throughout the Torah, when we receive commandments to be loving, thoughtful, and considerate of those who are at a disadvantage socially, emotionally, or financially, the commandments instruct us to do that because we must remember that we "were slaves in Mitzrayim." We can better understand and fulfill this commandment because of our own painful past.

REBIRTHING OURSELVES ...

Perhaps our traditional understanding that Miriam was a midwife gives us additional insight. Giving birth today is painful but was certainly more so in Miriam's time. But most women are willing to go through labor and delivery not only once, but repeatedly because what comes at the end of that pain, and (in fact) through that pain, are children. When we are willing to go through pain, we have the potential of giving birth to a new level of self that isn't possible without pain.

In addition, the pain the Jewish people suffered in Egypt would not have disappeared if they tried to ignore what happened. They could not have "just gotten over it." If you ask people who have suffered significantly in their lives whether they ever get over what happened to them, most will tell you, "No, I haven't." That's because pain is energy that takes up residence in us, unless we do something with it. Until pain is put to use and allowed to be transformed or transforming, it stays with us and weighs us down. When a person is described as "having a lot of baggage," this means the person never unpacked and put away or redirected the negative energy they were carrying around. The difference between wisdom and baggage is what we do with our pain. Do we wallow in it, or do we widen our horizons and grow from it?

Just as we learned that matza is the bread of redemption and the bread of affliction, God commands us to eat the maror, with its dual nature. We are to take the pain with us and use it to nourish our souls and enhance our wisdom. We usually describe the bite of maror as "strong." We can remember that what goes down "strong" can usually be strengthening.

LIGHTENING OUR LOAD ...

With the knowledge that pain can actually help us reach new levels of wisdom, our initial dread and fear of having pain in our lives can change to the feeling of pride and accomplishment that accompanies the eating of maror at the seder table. When we know what to do with our past, we don't have to keep carrying it around looking for a place to dump it. We can unpack, sort, put away, and use what we have to make us stronger. When we properly unpack our baggage, and we remember and live the lessons learned from a painful situation, we lighten our lives, take out the sting, and are left with the wisdom to continue a spiritually healthy journey through life.

LIFE IS BITTERSWEET ...

Further insight comes from the way we eat maror at our seder tables today. Before we eat it, we dip it into charoset, which, depending on your family's tradition, is made of chopped apples, nuts, cinnamon, and wine. Charoset symbolizes the mortar of the bricks the Jewish people were forced to make for Pharaoh in Egypt. The work for Pharaoh was grueling, and what made it worse was that it was futile. The sages teach us that the buildings the Jewish people built sank into the sand as soon as they were finished. Any bit of pride of accomplishment they could possibly have felt sank into the ground with their bricks.

The charoset we eat is always sweet. Building gives us pleasure when it serves a purpose. When we combine the bitterness of the maror with the sweetness of the charoset, we are literally ingesting the message that pain can lead to building us into greater people. We can recognize that pain is a necessary ingredient in our life and serves a purpose for our growth. This awareness, that life presents us with a bittersweet duality, enables us to stay in the present moment, without being distracted or distraught that we have difficulties in our life. This hard-earned knowledge allows us to extract the full potential for growth that exists in every situation.

KEEPING LIFE IN PERSPECTIVE ...

Another lesson from the charoset is that we should remember that when we are facing either small or significant challenges, there is always more on our plate than maror. It isn't the whole meal. There is also the sweet charoset. Pain may cry out and get most of our attention, but there are always other blessings and sources of sweetness in our lives that get overlooked or dismissed when we are in pain. "Dipping" our pain in some of the many blessings we have helps us keep our lives in perspective.

Bitter, not bad ...

One word you may have noticed missing from the description of maror is the word "bad." We've used the words "painful" and "bitter," but not "bad." That is because there is a big difference in what our attitude is toward something that we think of as being bitter or painful, versus bad. Saying that something is bitter or gives us pain is purely descriptive. There is no judgment involved in just describing how we experience something. It is the same as saying that something gave us pleasure or was sweet. The word "bad" is a judgment about the situation and implies that it is wrong, just as saying something is "good" implies that it is right.

Since we know there are many things that are pleasurable and sweet and are bad for us, it is reasonable to assume that there are also things that are painful and bitter that are good for us. Sweetness is no guarantee that it's good, and bitterness is no guarantee that it's bad. Living in the present moment means being able to say what our experience feels like to us without judging it. Since we have an aversion to things that are bad and try to avoid them, naming a potentially painful or bitter situation as bad can prevent us from growing from that experience. Our fear of things that we consider bad can also cause us to either avoid or deny the reality of what is going on at the moment. Pushing the maror off the plate, or pretending that it's not there, will never be the way to get through the seder or our lives. But adding charoset (our work and effort) to the maror (our difficult situation), will sweeten the bitterness and actually make us proud that we are able to eat it after all.

We entered the Passover Room and began with the alcoves devoted to matza and maror because they are central symbols of Passover and are mentioned specifically in the Torah to be incorporated into our seder. However, there is another unique part of the seder which we'll explore in the next alcove—the four cups of wine that God commands us to drink throughout the seder. We'll find out why there are four cups and why we recite a separate blessing on each one. What do these cups of wine have to teach us about living in the present moment?

FOUR CUPS OF WINE:
REDEMPTION UNFOLDING

Wine—our symbol of sanctification *and* joy—initiates all our festivals throughout the year, in addition to our weekly celebration of Shabbat. As we enter the next alcove, the table standing in the center has four full cups of wine on it, with a taller (but empty) fifth cup standing behind the four full cups. It appears to be a table prepared for at least four people, but, in fact, it isn't. These four cups are all for one person—they are for you. On Passover, our Festival of Redemption, we not only begin the holiday with Kiddush over wine, but throughout the seder we will repeat the blessing over wine (*borei p'ri hagafen*—Creator of the fruit of the vine) three more times and drink a full cup (if possible) with each new blessing.

One of the reasons this is so unusual is that normally when we make a blessing over food, we say the blessing only before we eat or drink the first portion. One blessing over wine at the beginning of a meal usually covers all the wine that we might drink throughout the meal. Why on Passover do we make four separate blessings, as if we hadn't already had the previous cup(s)? The answer to this question gives us insight into living in the present moment.

THE FOUR PHRASES AND PHASES ...

Each cup of wine symbolizes one of the four phrases and phases of redemption from Mitzrayim (Egyptian bondage) that God promises Moses before he agrees to accept the responsibility of leading the Jewish people. It is interesting that God makes the promise as a series of steps rather than as one sweeping statement. This tells us that it is God's desire that redemption unfolds in stages, and that it wasn't faulty planning that makes the process take so much time. The quote below from the Torah is God's description given to Moses about each of the stages of redemption and how the process would take place.

"Therefore say to the Children of Israel: 'I am Hashem (God), and I shall take you out from under the burdens of Egypt; I shall rescue you from their service; I shall redeem you with an outstretched arm and with great judgments. I shall take you to Me for a people and I shall be a God to you; and you shall know that I am Hashem your God, Who takes you out from under the burdens of Egypt. I shall bring you to the land about which I raised My hand to give it to Abraham, Isaac, and Jacob; and I shall give it to you as a heritage—I am Hashem.'"
– Exodus 6:6-8

As we can see, there were actually five different stages of our redemption:

1. I shall take you out from under the burdens of Egypt,

   (BEFORE LEAVING COUNTRY)
   6 mos BEFORE LEAVING

2. I shall rescue you from their service,

FREEDOM:
1) PHYSICALLY
2) EMOTIONALLY
3) SPIRITUALLY

IN METSCROLL COMMENTS

3. I shall redeem you with an outstretched arm and with great judgments,

4. I shall take you to Me for a people, and

5. I shall bring you to the land about which I raised My hand.

If the structure of the redemption process was significant for the grandest demonstration of national redemption of the entire Jewish people, it would be important to recognize and appreciate that it would also be the pattern for our own individual lives. Our lives unfold in stages; we are involved in a process of becoming that requires time. If God wanted to "beam up" the Jewish people from Egypt and "materialize" them in the Land of Israel with Torah in hand, that could have been done. Clearly, that isn't how things happened then, nor is it how things happen in our own lives either. Growing and developing into the person we are meant to become takes many steps.

CELEBRATING EACH STEP
ALONG THE WAY ...

Drinking four separate cups of wine throughout the Seder instills in us the reality that life progresses in stages and that we should accept whatever stage we are currently in. Because wine brings us joy, we are encouraged not only to accept our current stage but also to celebrate and bless it. If we feel discouraged because we're on cup number two rather than cup number four, that means we're missing the point and the opportunity to expe-

what

rience a sense of accomplishment about where we are right now.

On the other hand, we also tend to live in the future in a way that seems to be positive—always thinking about will happen in the next hour, the next day, or the next year. "I can't wait until five, when work will be over," or "I can't wait until my birthday, my graduation, your wedding, our vacation, etc." Since wherever we focus our minds is where we truly are, we often miss the opportunity to celebrate our current experience. We can wish our lives away, always looking for what's coming next. There's a common expression that we tend to think of as being positive, but which we need to be careful about: "I'm looking forward to ..." While it is great to have a vision and an optimistic sense of anticipation about our lives, we don't want to spend all of our time always looking forward instead of focusing on where we are right now. Just as some people set their watches ten minutes fast so they won't be late, some of us live our lives figuratively ten minutes ahead of where we are, so we're not present to what is actually happening to us. Having four cups of wine throughout the seder reminds us to stay focused on exactly where we are. We're not supposed to get excited about our fourth cup of wine while we're drinking our first.

EACH MOMENT IS COMPLETE IN ITS OWN WAY ...

Filling each cup and drinking the full amount in each one gives us another insight: each cup, and therefore each step, has its own completeness. It is tempting to slip into "future thinking," believing that happiness, contentment, or success will exist in the future when whatever we're waiting for has happened. By distracting us from the present moment, this way of thinking tends to keep happiness always out of reach because there's always something more that could be done. Drinking each cup of wine with joy reminds us to recognize each step along the way as being complete unto itself and worthy of acknowledgment and celebration.

The popular Passover song "Dayenu," which means "it would have been enough," expresses this same idea. Each verse of the song mentions one of the smaller steps involved in our redemption from Egypt and recognizes that the total redemption was made up of smaller redemptive moments. This song is sung looking back with perfect hindsight. Nevertheless, "Dayenu" says we are capable of perceiving that redemption is a process and *singing* our way through each step.

[handwritten margin notes: (NOT JUST "ENOUGH", BUT "ENOUGH FOR NOW" FOR ENCOURAGEMENT. ABOUT BEING GRATEFUL MOST IMPORTANT !!!)]

LET THE PROCESS FILL
YOU WITH JOY ...

We don't begin our Seder by guzzling all four cups of wine one after the next. Having the four cups spread out teaches us not to overwhelm ourselves with how much more is left to accomplish. We have no commandment to do everything all at once. Staying mindful of the cup that is in front of us brings us happiness now. We should remember that we are celebrating the process, which can be discouraging and difficult, with wine. Wine, by its nature, makes us feel physically relaxed and spiritually elevated. This teaches us that we can bless, drink, and savor each step along the way. We can trust that the potential that is being realized at any given moment is exactly what we have the ability to enjoy and drink in right now.

ELIJAH'S CUP ...

When we came into this alcove, we noticed that there was a fifth cup that stood empty behind the four filled cups. This is Elijah's cup. Elijah the Prophet, as most Jewish children can tell you, comes to everyone's home on seder night and drinks from the Elijah cup which is filled at the same time as the fourth cup after the Seder meal. Elijah is the harbinger of the messiah who represents the ultimate and final redemption. For now, only Elijah "drinks" from this fifth cup of wine because it represents the final promise that has not yet been fulfilled. Although we do not drink from this fifth cup, we fill it each year with trust that, just as the other four promises from God were kept, this one will be as well.

For each of us, filling Elijah's cup reminds us to trust and invest in the ongoing process of redemption and our own ongoing process of spiritual growth, even when our goal seems beyond our reach. The fifth and final full cup of wine that we associate with complete redemption is not yet ready for us to drink. The time of drinking may be in the future, but the time of pouring is here and now.

While we wait to be able to drink the fifth cup of redemption, the four cups of wine that we are able to drink keep us focused on and faithful to the continuous, redemptive process which we embrace and celebrate. The four cups of wine at our Passover Seder remind us to be fully present and joyful about each stage of redemption and growth, even while we recognize that there is much more left to accomplish.

One idea for us to keep in mind is that the process of redemption often hides from us in unexpected places and situations. We need to stay spiritually awake and attuned to the potential in every moment to search for, and hopefully find, the gems of opportunity that we know hide in our ordinary lives. The search for the *afikoman* at the end of the *Seder* epitomizes the alertness and enthusiasm that we need in this lifelong search, and it is the theme of our next and final alcove in the Passover Room.

SEEKING THE AFIKOMAN: THE THRILL OF THE SEARCH

Small children, and even those who are not so small, get excited to search for the *afikoman*, the half piece of matza that the Seder leader has wrapped and hidden at some point during the meal. The children individually, or in teams, scatter throughout the house to look for the afikoman in hopes of receiving a small prize for finding it. The thrill of the hunt wakes up those who had begun to get sleepy from the long Seder and meal. Where is it? Everyone has a theory about where the afikoman might be, and then they start asking for clues. Interestingly, no one comes right out and demands to be told exactly where it is. "Just give us a hint!" they plead. Very few children, if any, refuse to look. Knowing that something is hidden and waiting to be found— just like a game of "hide and seek"—triggers something in us and compels us to search. Like children seeking the afikoman, we are going to explore what it means to look for the hidden gifts that the present moment constantly gives us.

WHAT DOES THE AFIKOMAN REPRESENT?

As we turn the corner and enter the fourth and final alcove in the Passover Room, we see a space that is very different from the other rooms and alcoves we've been in. Because the afikoman is all about searching for what is hidden, there is nothing that can represent the afikoman other than places and situations where we are supposed to look for it. The afikoman represents searching for spiritual gifts that aren't apparent to us on the surface. It's easy to forget that within the challenges and blessings of everyday life lie Divine messages and opportunities for growth and transformation and ultimately redemption. The search for the afikoman is a powerful message and reminder for each of us—at every stage of life—to be on the lookout for all these hidden opportunities.

Therefore, when we come into this alcove, we are presented with a photographic collage that visually represents life's many moments and daily situations. On the surface, none of the pictures reveal anything out of the ordinary. These are moments we can all relate to. We see someone standing in the rain on the highway next to a car with a flat tire, people gathered in the park for a family BBQ, a young mother chasing after a crawling infant, a teenager arguing with her parents about weekend curfew, a man leaving his office after being let go because his company is downsizing, a woman hovering over the hospital bed of her sick father, a child's birthday party, an older person standing in a long line at the grocery store, or a woman standing at the kitchen counter cutting vegetables for her dinner. These are snippets of life's everyday moments—pleasant, annoying, exciting, sad, and just plain ordinary. Our days are filled with moments like these. How does knowing about afikoman give us a way to encounter these mundane times and search for something special within them?

THE PRESENT MOMENT, LIKE OUR AFIKOMAN, IS A PRESENT ... AND COMES GIFT-WRAPPED

We can find many different insights about living in the present moment with this one scenario of searching for the afikoman. We've looked at the meanings of Hebrew words before, but here, English words help us too. Usually, when someone gives us a present, it is wrapped in some way. Even if it is concealed only in part with simple wrapping and a bow, presents normally are *presented* to us covered. The afikoman is always wrapped before it is hidden, whether in a paper napkin or a fancy, official "afikoman bag." The afikoman is a present.

The present moment, like the afikoman, is also a present and comes to us in the same way—concealed. We have to remove the wrapping in order to get to the gift inside. Have you ever given someone something wrapped up that didn't bring a smile to his or her face? We like things that are hidden; they intrigue us. When we apply the same principle to our lives and recognize that we need to and are willing to "unwrap" the moment to see what it really holds for us, the pleasure of the afikoman, and the search for it, can be with us year-round.

THE AFIKOMAN IS HIDDEN ALSO ...

The afikoman, however, is not only wrapped, but it is also hidden. A person has to expend significant effort to go looking for it and find it. This is also like the present moment, which we must investigate in order to determine what we are supposed to do with it. Always looking for our afikoman describes a way of looking at life as requiring an ongoing search and exploration.

GOD GIVES US HINTS ...

Living in the present moment means being highly aware that the afikoman is hidden and knowing there are clues about where to find it. The clues we have for finding the afikoman in our lives are the ideas that we've talked about in the other alcoves and in other rooms: wisdom from the past—where has the afikoman been before—and a vision of the future—we're looking with the lights on instead of in the dark. Wouldn't it be unfortunate if a child at a Passover Seder didn't even bother to look for the afikoman because he thought that because he couldn't see it in plain view, it wasn't there, or if no one had told him it was hidden and he was supposed to look for it? At the heart of the search for the afikoman is a fundamental premise: we trust that the Seder leader has indeed hidden the afikoman and it is not a cruel joke that we're looking for something that isn't there. In our lives, we trust that the ultimate Seder leader—God—wraps and hides the afikoman for us, knows where it is, and gives us hints so we can find it.

UNWRAPPING THE MOMENT ...

Living in the present moment is exciting. Just look at the beaming face of a child who has found the half piece of matza wrapped in a napkin. Had it been out on the table for all to see, no one would have been interested. That it was wrapped and hidden and required a search made it worth everything. It is the uncertainty, which we usually want to avoid in our lives, that also creates the excitement. Living in the present moment means we are living with uncertainty but trusting the process of the search and having confidence that the afikoman will be found. And it means being able to ask ourselves the question, "I wonder if I 'unwrap' this moment, what I will find?" The moment is disguised: it looks like an ordinary situation or an unwelcome challenge, but what does the moment hold for me? Will I find that it's really an opportunity to grow in patience, express compassion, demonstrate perseverance, or maintain integrity? What's the spiritual prize inside? Do we recognize that the Creator of the Universe has given each of us a life in which we have the potential to blossom and grow and that each challenge along the way is designed specifically to stimulate our spiritual growth? Can we become more aware and sensitive to the reality that if it were left up to us, we'd probably never challenge our own spiritual development?

As noted earlier, we call the service and meal that we conduct and partake of on Passover a seder. "Seder" means "order" and is perhaps the most fundamental idea to take with us from this Passover Room. This celebration is called a "seder" for many reasons, but an important insight to remember is that Passover celebrates our redemption from Mitzrayim. Redemption from Mitzrayim, as well as the final redemption of humanity, takes place in a certain order that God has determined. Even though there are an infinite variety of *Hagaddahs*, which people use to conduct their Seders, all of them proceed in the same order. When we hold a Seder, we act out our belief that there is order in Creation and order in how the purpose of Creation and the purpose of our own lives are unfolding. From our limited human perspective, when redemption is hidden and our own personal path is unclear, it is easy to think there is no order and redemption and answers cannot be found. The concepts related to the afikoman—it is wrapped, hidden, searched for, and found—seem to be related to a world of the unknown and disorder rather than to order. The fact that the afikoman is placed within the context and framework of the Seder tells us, though, that although there are moments that appear to us as signs of disorder, there is a grand order that surrounds and encompasses our lives at all times. We can trust and feel confident that God is indeed the ultimate Seder Leader. When we do, we will begin to discover and appreciate the order and meaning that is hidden within our challenges of living.

It's all a gift

Every moment is a gift. Some moments are given to us simply concealed in plain paper, others are stashed away in dark closets, some are wrapped in odd-shaped boxes, and others may come humorously wrapped in last week's comics. Nonetheless, they are all gifts for us to search for and unwrap. How many presents we search for and unwrap each day is always our choice. The true gift is to know they are there waiting for us.

The celebrations we learned about in the Holiday Room and the Passover Room and their rituals that heighten our awareness provide us with a wealth of insight and inspiration to use throughout the year, long after the holiday has passed. What can help us stay focused when there are no holidays? We are blessed to have a number of *mitzvot* (commandments that connect us to God) that help us cultivate a present-moment perspective on a daily basis and that echo the lessons that we learn from celebrating each of our holidays. The holidays and the mitzvot are our divine design. Together they create a framework and a structure that continuously center us and guide us as we flourish and grow throughout the year in our House of the Present Moment. We'll now move into the Mitzvot Room, so we can share four different mitzvot that connect us to building a life that flows with strength and vitality.

V.

Mitzvot Room

INTRODUCTION

THE SPIRITUAL OPPORTUNITIES that each holiday gives us to practice different aspects of living in the present moment are particularly rich, be it the active trust of Chanukah that gives us courage to face overwhelming odds with seemingly limited resources or the passive trust of Sukkot that invites us to seek spiritual security, rather than chasing physical safety and certainty. However, except for Rosh Chodesh, which occurs monthly, all the other holidays are once-a-year events.

How are we supposed to hold on to the gift of spiritual insights that we gain with each of these holidays until they come again? Is there some way to capture the moment and bring it with us? Fortunately, we have been given the gift of *mitzvot* or command-

(SEE APPENDIX)

ments. While it is true that the mitzvot have been commanded of us, to call them "commandments," as if they were a list of extraneous orders to be carried out in a sterile and robotic way, is to miss the more essential, deeper purpose of mitzvot completely. The word mitzvot is related to the word "*tzav*," which means to connect or attach. This is truly what mitzvot do. They connect us to God, other people, ourselves, and the world around us. A mitzvah is like a lifeline because it has the ability, using every day and ordinary events and situations, to make us fully aware of the gifts that await us in every moment.

CAPTURING THE MOMENT
EVERY DAY ...

While there are some mitzvot that are like holidays and only performed on an occasional basis, we're going to explore mitzvot that we can perform daily and that help us focus on and live in the present more frequently and successfully. Since we are physical, spiritual, emotional, intellectual, and verbal beings, we need to fill our House of the Present Moment with actions, rituals, feelings, thoughts, and words to create a vibrant place to dwell and grow.

Join us as we enter the Mizvot Room. We'll begin in the first alcove, where we see an enormous, clear, glass box filled with bills and coins and engraved with the word "*Tzedakah*" or charity, across its front. What is this collection of money all about?

TZEDAKAH:
IN GOD WE TRUST

Many of us remember growing up in homes with tzedakah boxes in them. Whether our family collected money for Israel, a local Jewish organization, or some other worthy cause, the idea of giving money to charity is a familiar concept to us. There's also something deeper about the mitzvah of tzedakah that cultivates a spiritual state of being conducive to living in the present moment.

The word "tzedakah," while often translated as "charity," doesn't really mean that at all. Charity comes from the Latin "*caritas*" and means "to care." *Tzedakah* literally means "righteousness" or "justice." This doesn't mean that we don't care; it means that tzedakah has a deeper purpose for both the giver and the receiver.

Giving tzedakah is about establishing righteousness and justice for the recipient. The Torah teaches us that 10% of the money we have does not belong to us. It has been given to us in trust to distribute to those in need. The money actually belongs to the eventual recipients; we are only the vehicles of its distribution. It's similar to sales tax, which stores collect on behalf of the city or state. The money is in their cash register, but it doesn't belong to them. They are obligated to remit the taxes collected to the appropriate governmental unit. Money comes to us in the same way: 90% is for us and 10% comes through us but isn't for us. That's why giving tzedakah is about righteousness and justice more than it is about caring. Of course, caring enhances the mitzvah and elevates the giving to a higher level, but it isn't a prerequisite.

CHANGING THE WAY WE UNDERSTAND OUR MONEY ...

How does giving tzedakah, other than making us righteous and just people, help us live in the present moment? It doesn't seem to have anything to do with it. We need, though, to look at tzedakah from the giver's perspective. How people deal with their money often presents a clue about what their attitude is toward life. If we're trying to change our attitude toward life, changing the way we think of our money is a great way to help that happen.

Specifically, what does how we think about money reveal about us? One thing it tells us is how much trust we have—in life, in God, and in ourselves. People, for example, who lived through the Depression or other serious financial difficulties, may have very different attitudes toward money and life. They often don't trust either one. Their response may be to hoard money, or what money can buy, in an attempt to buy safety. This lack of trust is based on fear—fear of not having enough. While their personal experience in the past was real and frightening, their past continues to haunt them and causes them to react to current situations as if those were the same as past ones. This is human nature, but it is an obstacle to living in the present moment. The present may or may not be similar to a past situation. Automatically reacting as if it were the same keeps a person locked in the past, instead of bringing the past to the present by using the wisdom gained from previous experiences to accurately evaluate current situations.

Money is all about flow. Economic models discuss the flow of money through the system. Whether the economy is "sluggish" or "heating up too fast," for example, are questions economists ask about money. "Consumer confidence" (read: "trust") has an enormous impact on the health of the economy. Each of us is also an economic system and money is supposed to flow through us as well. Our lack of trust will lead us to hoard money that doesn't belong to us and clog up our system, in addition to hurting the economic system on which tzedakah is based.

In the United States, we're fortunate that our money has engraved on it for us to see every time we use it: "In God We Trust." What a perfect reminder. We need to know that God has given us money in trust—He trusts that we'll remit what isn't ours and that we'll trust that what remains is what we are supposed to have for ourselves. The challenge is that most people really feel they can't "afford" to give tzedakah because they perceive that all the money that has flowed into their account is theirs and is for their own use. Most of us try to hang on to our money as much as possible. After all, "I worked hard for my money and it's mine." This is our response when we don't yet understand what tzedakah really is. It causes us to miss the spiritual opportunity to cultivate trust and happily, even eagerly, give the right amount of tzedakah and participate in the flow of life itself.

STAYING IN THE CURRENT ...

It's also helpful to notice that money is called "currency," which reminds us of *water currents* flowing smoothly, as well as of the word "current," which means what is happening right now. Having a visible tzedakah box to put money into every day can slowly change the way we perceive the money that comes to us. Being part of the flow of money encourages us to take our tzedakah-giving as a serious spiritual pursuit designed to benefit us as givers as much as the recipients.

Even though we certainly can give tzedakah using checks and credit cards, there is something uniquely satisfying about putting coins or bills into a tzedakah box. Our hands are for giving; when we handle the money directly, there is a greater sense that we are personally involved. Plus, for some reason, everyone likes the sound of coins dropping into, and the look of, a tzedakah box filling up. Each time we put money into a tzedakah box, we can feel the pleasure of expansiveness. Do you know anyone who looks at his or her filled tzedakah box and says, "Look how much money I've lost to tzedakah?" The natural response—even of young children—is "Look how much money *I have* in my tzedakah box." Money they know is not for them.

GIVING LEADS TO WEALTH ...

Interestingly, our tradition has a wonderful commentary on the mitzvah of tzedakah. The tradition is stated in the Torah, where we are commanded to tithe (which means to give 10%) in Deuteronomy 14:22. The wording says *"aser t'aser,"* which means, "You shall surely tithe." Because of the way words are written in the Torah—without the dots and vowels—these same words can be read as *"aser t'asher"* which means "tithe and you shall become wealthy." While living in the present moment does not promise to bring us great material wealth, there is something to be said for first recognizing how God has created the world as a complete physical-spiritual system, and then participating in it. The reason that someone, by giving tzedakah, can become wealthy and not poor as our fears would often have us believe, is because God gives us our livelihood in trust. If we earn $1,000 and know that only $900 belongs to us and the remaining $100 is to be remitted to tzedakah, we become worthy of God's greater trust. Just as a parent is more likely to give a child who is responsible with his or her allowance a bigger allowance, so too is God more likely to give us more money in total when we use it as He commands. God's goals are twofold: the poor must receive their money and the givers need to learn to trust that God is the source of their wealth and their giving will not lead to their impoverishment. If the poor get their money more readily from us, and we demonstrate our trust by giving it willingly and in a timely way, we are better trustees for more money from God. Perhaps next year we'll get $10,000 because God trusts that we won't hesitate to remit the $1,000. It is partly this reasoning that leads to everyone's obligation, even those who are poor, to participate in giving tzedakah. Their tzedakah may be part of their path out of poverty.

OUR MONEY IS LIKE MANNA ...

Tzedakah incorporates the lesson of the manna in the desert that we experience on Shabbat, as well as the lesson of the sukkah that we build and dwell in throughout Sukkot. We both see and digest the lesson of the two loaves of challah on Shabbat, which teaches us to trust that God is the source of the physical nourishment we need and to trust that it is always being provided. So too, does the mitzvah of tzedakah teach us to trust the flow of sustenance in the form of money. Sitting in the sukkah teaches us that spiritual security should be our aspiration, rather than the unreachable goal of guaranteed physical safety. The mitzvah of tzedakah reinforces the lesson of the sukkah. It helps to wean us from the mistaken belief that hanging on to our money will make us safe. As we practice giving tzedakah, we come to realize that it is what we give, not what we hold onto, that makes us most secure. Shabbat comes once a week and Sukkot comes once a year. Having a daily mitzvah that reinforces the deep insights these holidays bring us increases the opportunities we have to practice living in the present moment.

The power and message of the huge tzedakah box in this alcove now becomes clear. With each coin or dollar we drop into the tzedakah box, we can focus on three essential ideas: God has given us money that really belongs to other people, trusting us to give it to them rather than keep it all for ourselves. As we participate in the daily flow of currency, we are part of the current flow of life and are not stuck in the past. And finally, we can trust that our giving money now will not impoverish us in the future—in fact, it could make us richer.

Coin by coin, dollar by dollar, day by day, the mitzvah of tzedakah slowly rewires our thinking and our perceptions. The way we relate to our money speaks volumes about the way we relate to our lives. Our goal is to have the saying "In God We Trust" transform us and move from just words engraved on our money to a belief that is engraved in our hearts and practiced with our hands. So, take a coin and drop it in.

In addition to tzedakah, there is another mitzvah that gives us the opportunity to redefine and refine our perspective of ourselves on a daily basis. That mitzvah is the commandment of *teshuvah*, which means to return. It is the focus of our next alcove.

TESHUVAH: TODAY IS THE FIRST DAY OF THE REST OF YOUR LIFE

The next mitzvah we will explore requires no physical objects and can be done whenever and wherever we want. It is probably the mitzvah that will affect our lives most profoundly, and it is the one that epitomizes both the path and the ability to live in the present moment. The mitzvah of *teshuvah* is often translated as repentance but really means "to return." Teshuvah's returning is a returning to ourselves, to the true person created in the image of God, who we were meant to be.

As we round the corner and enter this next alcove, we see that all of the room's walls are mirrors. As we walk in, we start to catch images of ourselves reflecting off each wall. At first, it's a little disconcerting to see ourselves from so many angles at one time; then, almost out of curiosity, we begin to really look. It is this ability to observe ourselves from many angles that symbolizes the ability to see ourselves clearly without hiding or pushing unpleasant aspects of ourselves to the back, where they won't be noticed.

FACING THE PARADOX OF DENIAL
AND DEFENSIVENESS ...

People are usually only willing to do this careful introspection if they don't feel threatened. What threatens us? We feel threatened when we think that we, or who we believe ourselves to be, are under attack. This happens whenever we over-identify with our actions and behaviors that are incorrect and believe that they are the "real us." This occurs when over-identification with our mistakes and confusion about who the "real me" is cause us to engage in a self-defeating process of denial and defensiveness. If I *am* my mistake, then I have to either deny it to protect myself from attack or I have to defend it in order to remain righteous in my own eyes. We unwittingly create the paradox of holding onto a behavior that we've accepted as our identity, even when we don't like it. With denial, we'll never be able to correct the behavior, and with defensiveness, we don't want to. In either case, no change is possible, and we imprison ourselves within a self-created, artificial identity.

The power of teshuvah is in the recognition that we are *not* our behaviors to a great extent, our behaviors are external to our real selves and to our souls, and we can discard them once we discover them. If someone tells us or we notice that there is mud on our new silk dress, our distress is about the fact that we've soiled a beautiful and valuable garment. We wouldn't tell another person or ourselves that either the mud wasn't there or that the mud was supposed to be there. In fact, if someone pointed it out to us, we'd probably be grateful to know, so that we could take care of cleaning it up as soon as possible.

SEEING THE BEAUTY BENEATH
THE SURFACE ...

When someone has a teshuvah-consciousness, it means he or she can always see that the moment or the situation could be different than it has been in the past. We can clean up the mud and restore the silk dress to its original beauty because the beauty was always there. Taking a good look in the mirror isn't just to see the spots. We want to see the beautiful dress—our beauty and goodness—as the context for our teshuvah. To look at the dress and only see the mud spots is to miss the point completely.

Every morning in Judaism's daily prayers, there is a blessing that reminds us of the purity of our souls:

"My God, the soul You placed within me is pure. You created it, You fashioned it, You breathed it into me, You safeguard it within me, and eventually, You will take it from me, and restore it to me in Time to Come. As long as the soul is within me, I gratefully thank You, Hashem, my God and the God of my forefathers, Master of all works, Lord of all souls. Blessed are You, God, Who restores souls to dead bodies."
(Morning blessings)

Lest we think we're old *shmattahs* (rags), this blessing reminds us that all of us have pure souls—silk dresses—entrusted to us for safekeeping during our lives. As anyone who has ever owned a silk dress knows, we need to take them to the cleaners often—and it's expensive to keep them looking nice.

This is true, too, with our souls, which are our true selves. We need to exert effort to keep them pure. We always need to strive to return to our purest, cleanest state of being. This is the process of teshuvah. Unlike dropping a garment at the dry cleaners, however, we need to stay personally involved in the return and cleansing of the "mud" that gets stuck to our souls.

WHAT ARE THE STEPS?

There are four steps in the cleansing process. Lori Palatnik, a prominent Jewish lecturer and author, summarizes these steps into a variation of the well-known acronym RSVP. We all know that when an invitation comes with an RSVP, it means we're supposed to respond. When situations for teshuvah come our way, we are also supposed to respond. But we change the order of the letters. Switching the "R" and the "S" we get SRVP, which stands for Stop, Regret, Verbalize, and Plan.

The teshuvah process begins by having the courage to stop. We need to Stop saying, doing, and thinking about the things that are self-destructive and that are keeping us from being our true selves. This step requires an awareness that even though what we have been doing has become habitual, it still isn't intrinsic to who we really are.

We also need to Regret that we have been self-destructive and untrue to ourselves. This means overcoming the tendency to become insensitive to what we are doing, and instead allow the implications of our actions—be they in the realm of speech, action, or thought—to really penetrate our hearts and minds. It isn't arrogant to think and even to say to ourselves, *"This behavior or thought is really unbecoming of someone as special and as important as I am."* Regret also may include apologizing to anyone who we affected with our actions and making restitution, if possible. Making other people whole who we have hurt by our actions is a prerequisite for making ourselves whole again.

Verbalizing what we have done wrong may seem to be unnecessary in this whole process, but that is the next step. It makes a big difference in our effectiveness. What we say creates a reality, even if it only makes more concrete one of the thousands of thoughts that constantly run through our minds. How do we know which thoughts we really believe? The thoughts that we articulate are more significant. In a courtroom situation, a plea bargain may require the defendant to verbally say what he or she did, as part of the deal. Something happens when we speak aloud. For teshuvah, we are lucky we don't have to appear in a courtroom, nor do we always have to verbalize to anyone else. We just have to say it so we can hear it. Even that isn't so easy to do.

The final stage of the cleansing process is to make a Plan for not repeating the mistake. This takes a lot of introspection and self-knowledge. What were the situations or triggers that created the environment in which this mistake became so easy to make? Why do I keep making the same mistake over and over again? Dieters know that they must plan how they will eat at a party to avoid unconscious overeating. When a person fails to realize that by standing close to the dessert table with a big plate they will likely overeat, it's almost certain that their most sincere desire to change and behave in a new way will be sabotaged. Einstein once said, "Insanity is doing the same thing over and over again and expecting different results." This final stage of *teshuvah's* cleansing process, having a plan, increases the chances that our commitment to beginning anew will succeed.

Keeping these four letters and the steps they represent in mind can help us stay focused on the reality that every moment is an invitation to return to our true selves. We just need to RSVP with our SRVP.

Whether it is a small habit of speech, a fleeting thought, an infrequent behavior, or something much bigger that is getting in the way of our living as our true selves, the process and power of teshuvah can help us clean up the "mud" from our pure "silk" souls. We have the additional benefit of our tradition teaching us that God is the ultimate cleaner. While a silk dress can come back still with a shadow of the stain, God removes all traces of stain once we have gone through the steps that are ours to take.

KEEPING THE "HIGH" OF THE HIGH HOLIDAYS ...

While many of us *do* think about the process of teshuvah at Rosh Hashanah and Yom Kippur, the mitzvah of teshuvah gives us the opportunity to go through the exact same process at any moment throughout the year. Every time we do, we bring ourselves fully into the present moment and have access to some of the "high" of the High Holidays. When we recognize our inherent purity and realize that our past mistakes and missteps do not define us, we will want to go through the necessary cleansing steps so that we can be restored to our true selves and be fully present to the potential that awaits us. The "Teshuvah Cleaners" is open all day, every day.

How can we remember that this teshuvah process is available to us in our daily lives? When there isn't an actual holiday to help remind us, we get caught up in the normal, busy routine of living. Are there some physical means that are easily accessible to us that will help us to remember to engage in this ongoing cleansing process? In our next alcove, we invite you to learn about a simple ritual that we can naturally incorporate into our daily way of life. We're fortunate that there is something that is so easy to do that can bring us such great awareness.

SPIRITUAL CLEANSING:
THE WAY OF WATER

If only cleansing ourselves and returning to our pure, most essential selves were as easy to do as taking a dress to the cleaners. The truth is, it is our lifelong challenge and the cleansing process is ongoing. Much like physical fitness, it isn't something that we achieve at last and then can take off our list of things to do. Spiritual cleansing and refocusing, which sounds inspiring, is a difficult idea to hang onto throughout our day-to-day lives. Fortunately, our tradition has a very down-to-earth way of building this awareness into our day.

If you were asked to think of what comes to mind when you think of cleansing, the answer would probably be "water." Indeed, water is the central focus of several mitzvot that remind us of the need for cleansing ourselves of stains and problems that constantly arise. Water is the agent and the metaphor for keeping the avenues of awareness open and flowing.

In the next alcove, we see and hear only water. Like the fountain in the center of Miriam's Courtyard, this alcove is built around a gently flowing fountain. A waist-high marble counter surrounds this fountain, so we can get up close to the water. Large copper cups, filled with the fountain's water to pour over our hands, are on the counter. Our hands, which symbolize our ability to act and do in the world, are the focus of almost all of the mitzvot that involve water.

Everything that we learned about water in Miriam's Courtyard comes together for us here. We remember that almost all of Miriam's stories were connected to water in one way or another. Mayim, water, reminds us that there is always a hidden flow even in Mitzrayim, the constricted, difficult, and painful situations that we all face. The mitzvot that use water as part of their observance all have an underlying connection and help us relate to and integrate the insights we discovered while in Miriam's Courtyard. Specifically, the teshuva process is only possible when we are in a state of flow—like water—and are open to the Divine possibilities of the moment.

WAKING UP AND
BEGINNING THE DAY ...

As soon as we wake up in the morning, our tradition teaches us to take a washing cup and pour water over our hands to separate ourselves from spiritual impurities that attach to us during sleep. Sleeping, while completely essential to our health, is also considered to bring us to a state of being that is slightly death-like because we are taught that while we sleep, our souls partially leave us.

Given that our goal is to always embrace life, we take even a slight brush with death seriously. Ritually washing our hands each morning reminds us that we have been brought back to life for a brand-new day. The washing further encourages us to consider how much more concern we should have about the choices we make in our attitudes and actions during the wakeful part of the day. We want to stay away from actions that might be "death-like" if they pull us in a self-defeating or self-destructive way. We begin each day mindfully, with a ritual of pouring water over each hand. This action reminds us to separate from anything that dulls us and to open the gift of a new day with gratitude, hope, and commitment to making our *renewed* life a purposeful one.

You might wonder if taking a good hot shower or soaking in a luxurious bath wouldn't accomplish the same thing. While either of these acts will make us feel wonderful—either refreshed or relaxed—our tradition teaches us that we receive something more, a Divine gift, when we pour water over our hands in the morning with the right focus and intention. We aren't required to go find some magical well in a far off or mystical place in order to effect this kind of spiritual cleansing. We have the opportunity to perform this ritual every day, wherever we are.

PHYSICAL NEEDS CREATE SPIRITUAL OPPORTUNITIES ...

The Torah and Judaism guide us in very practical ways. In addition to washing our hands ritually when we wake up in the morning, we also do the ritual throughout the day and any time we use the bathroom. (Ritual hand-washing comes, of course, after washing our hands with soap and water for hygienic reasons.) This mitzvah pretty much guarantees that at least several times a day we will have the opportunity to become mindful of our spiritual goals. We enhance and center our mindfulness with specific blessings that call our attention to what we are doing and what we are trying to accomplish. What could be a better metaphor for letting go and keeping ourselves clean of spiritual toxins than the ritual of hand-washing after our body has rid itself of physical toxins? The blessing we recite after this hand-washing refers to God as the one who "heals all flesh" because it is true that the miraculous ability of our body to remove physical waste keeps us healthy and represents a kind of healing. This preservation of our physical health is parallel to the ability of teshuvah to restore us to spiritual health. God has given us a normal physically functioning process through our bodily systems. That creates a constant reminder of the possibilities that also exist to be restored to spiritual good health.

ELEVATING OUR MUNDANE ACT OF EATING ...

Water comes into play again when we eat our meals. At any meal throughout the day, when bread is going to be eaten, ritual hand-washing precedes the meal. Even if it is a humble peanut butter and jelly sandwich, eating bread means we stop and wash before we begin to eat that sandwich. In this situation, we are washing our hands in imitation of the *Kohanim* (the Priests), who would wash before they made offerings on the altar in the Holy Temple.

Because we consider our tables to have a similar status to the altar in the Temple, and the food we eat to have the potential to bring us closer to God just as the Temple offerings did, we wash before we officiate at our tables. When we wash our hands, the blessing we say refers to "taking up our hands," meaning to elevate them. The sanctification of our table happens when we focus on eating as a means of giving us the energy to reach our spiritual potential, rather than just as an end unto itself. With this spiritual orientation, our meal takes on an entirely different meaning and purpose.

Our day doesn't need to be extraordinary to be spiritually uplifting. Before we ever do anything that we would consider to be "important," the daily needs of getting up, going to the bathroom, and eating have given us the opportunity to recognize what we are really in this world to do. Woven through an ordinary day are reminders to cleanse and elevate ourselves, to be present and open to the amazing potential for transformation that exists within each moment.

SANCTIFYING OUR RELATIONSHIPS ...

Thus far, we've only spoken about the mitzvot related to water that involve hand-washing. There is another water mitzvah that involves the entire body. This is the mitzvah of *mikveh*. Even though this mitzvah applies only to women in specific circumstances—married and menstruating—it is a mitzvah that is a cornerstone of Jewish life.

The *mikveh* is a pool of naturally collected water that women immerse in seven days after their menstrual flow has ceased. Immersion in a mikveh is done before a woman can resume sexual relations with her husband following her menstrual cycle. Just as we wash hands in the morning after sleeping because we have experienced a brush with death, so too the woman whose egg

169

was not fertilized and is menstruating also experiences a brush with death, and therefore needs ritual purification. The reality is the potential life that existed in her egg did not come to fruition; unrealized potential is always similar to death, regardless of whether or not a woman wanted to be pregnant.

WATERS OF HOPE ...

If that is so with an egg's potential, how much more so is it true for us? When we miss opportunities to realize our own potential because we have let ourselves become bogged down by our past or have become immobilized by our fears of the future, we experience a mini-death. Interestingly, the word *"mikveh"* has two meanings that can be connected. *"Mikveh"* means both "a gathering of water" and "hope." Completely immersing our bodies in the gathered waters of the mikveh gives us hope— hope for renewal and rebirth. In fact, when we emerge from the mikveh water, we are considered reborn and we are renewed. We are ready to focus again on realizing our life's potential.

For those who aren't in the marital or time-of-life stage that requires mikveh, there is the opportunity to immerse in the mikveh before Yom Kippur. On the Day of Atonement, all of us are considered reborn, and many have the custom of immersing in a mikveh in the days just before Yom Kippur to symbolize the transformation with which God gifts us on this holiday.

Staying in the flow of life isn't easy. There are a lot of eddies and whirlpools that can pull us off course and turn us around, as well as slippery stones and hidden logs that can trip us or catch us along the way. But being in the flow of water, which is the flow of life, is the only way to get where we want to go. Keeping the flow of water on our hands and in our minds throughout the day helps us to remember that we want to be in the flow, that we want to remove any barriers to that flow, and that we want to stay focused on navigating the waters that are our life's journey.

The ability to cleanse ourselves, and then to elevate and transform our potential into a reality, requires tremendous awareness and attention. The spiritual power of water is activated when it flows over our hands from a cup or when we immerse in a mikveh. We have the ability to recognize that the power of water is designed to slowly, but very surely, change us whenever we awaken to a new day, remove the toxins in our bodies, and get nourishment through the food that we eat.

The power of water symbolizes the power to change, and the power to change is the power to grow. Growth is the essence of life. The opportunities for growth depend on a number of different factors. In our fourth and final alcove in the Mizvot Room, we will discover one of those significant factors that guide us. We will learn about the mitzvah of *mezuzah*, and come to appreciate a commandment that provides us with a constant reminder of, and will call our attention to, the dynamic and ever-changing flow of our lives.

MEZUZAH:
SACRED SPACES IN ALL PLACES

As we enter our next alcove, we will pass through an archway with a *mezuzah* made of Jerusalem stone. A *mezuzah* is a small, narrow case, only several inches long, that contains a scroll with specific verses from the Torah inscribed on it. While all the rooms and alcoves in our House of the Present Moment are graced with mezuzahs, this one in the Mezuzah Alcove is larger and more distinctive. The mezuzah is always placed on the right-hand side of the doorway, slanting inward toward what is considered the more important space. We'll learn more about this as we continue. First, we will pause and focus on the mezuzah itself. You might be familiar with the obligation to have a mezuzah on the doorpost of our front door. However, the Torah teaches us that we are also to put mezuzahs on every doorpost within our homes (excluding the bathroom door). Why should that be? Isn't that going overboard? Isn't it enough to have one at the front door of our house?

Zooz! move!

We can glean a number of insights into this mitzvah by knowing what the word "mezuzah" means and the significance of how and where the mezuzah is placed. The root of the word "mezuzah" is "*zooz*," which means "to move." Even in English, the letter "Z" has a sound of movement and energy—a buzz. The word itself is calling our attention to the idea of movement. In Israel, if someone calls out to you, "Zooz!" it is usually accompanied by a raised voice and it means, "Move! Now!" The mezuzah is telling us the same thing—without the yelling. It is reminding us to keep moving forward—now.

The mezuzah is a small object with a big message. Subtly instilled in us through the awareness of the mezuzahs placed on all the doorways throughout our homes, is the reminder to move with the flow of life and what it presents to us at any given time.

THE POWER OF COMPROMISE ...

There was a debate about how the mezuzah should be placed on the doorway. Should it be vertical or horizontal? What's the best way? In many Jewish legal decisions, one way needs to be chosen, and it's not possible to compromise. However, with the mitzvah of mezuzah, a compromise position was possible. The compromise was that the mezuzah is placed on an angle, with its top slanted in toward the room we are entering. This placement alone hints at two things.

The first message of the diagonal placement of the mezuzah is that most relationships and situations require some sort of give and take and some sort of compromise, and that finding a new third way can hold the best qualities of both positions. It is a synthesis. A diagonal line moves up and across simultaneously and incorporates the essential qualities of vertical and horizontal lines at the same time. When we live in relationships, the mezuzah reminds us that there is often a third way that incorporates the essence of what both people want. Insisting on being only "horizontal" or only "vertical" can get us stuck and will keep us from moving through the door.

THE DIAGONAL DYNAMIC ...

The second insight that comes from the diagonal placement of the mezuzah is that in design, a diagonal line is always considered the most dynamic. It conveys movement, more than either a vertical or horizontal line alone can, probably because it has both kinds of movement incorporated into it. The diagonal placement of the mezuzah reminds us that life is always dynamic; nothing in time and/or space stays the same. Things are always changing, and life presents new opportunities, even when we walk from one room to the next in our own home. Our awareness of the mezuzah can also remind us that even within the same space, possibilities for change and, therefore, growth and hope exist. Because people tend to be to be visually oriented, we find it difficult to relate to the idea that there is a new opportunity in a space that looks the same as it did ten minutes ago, yesterday, or last week. The mezuzah reminds us of what we tend to forget: our environment, even when seemingly familiar, is not stagnant and is really a magical sea of movement.

Walking through the doorway
of possibility ...

That mezuzahs are to be put on doorways, rather than on walls, also tells us something. Doorways are specific structures that indicate we are moving from one room to another. Although we take them for granted, every time we move from one room to another, there is an entirely different set of unique possibilities that exists in that space. The choices we have in our kitchens are different than the choices we have in our bedrooms. The challenges we face in public differ from the challenges we have in our private lives. Being mindful of our mezuzahs aids us in becoming more sensitive to the subtle, as well as the more dramatic, differences and opportunities that are constantly unfolding before us.

So far, we've only talked about the external aspects of the mezuzah—what the word means, where it is supposed to be placed, and how it is supposed to look on the doorway.

As interesting as the external aspects of the mezuzah are, it is the inside scroll and what is written on it that has the vision and direction we are seeking to permeate throughout our homes and integrate into our lives. Since the words of the Torah give us vision and direction, so do the words of the mezuzah, which are taken directly from the Torah.

Since the mezuzah scroll is rolled up inside its holder, we usually don't see it and it is easy to forget what it looks like and what it says. Once we pass through the doorway of our alcove with the mezuzah on its doorpost, we see that the walls that surround us have the opening verses of the mezuzah text enlarged and displayed on the walls. A scribe wrote the text, using the same beautiful calligraphy that has been used to write Torah scrolls throughout the world and throughout time. Underneath the exhibited parchments are English translations of the verses. Let's look at some select phrases and examine their meaning, so we can understand how the mitzvah of mezuzah helps us live in the present moment.

In order to appreciate the context of these phrases, the sacred words of the opening text of the mezuzah appear below in both Hebrew and English.

שמע ישראל יקוק אלקנו יקוק אחד
ואהבת את יקוק אלקיך בכל לבבך ובכל נפשך ובכל מאדך
והיו הדברים האלה אשר אנכי מצוך היום על לבבך וש־
ננתם לבניך ודברת בם בשבתך בביתך ובלכתך בדרך ובש־
כבך ובקומך וקשרתם לאות על ידך והיו לטטפת בין עיניך
וכתבתם על מזזות ביתך ובשעריך

Here, Israel, Hashem is our God, Hashem, the One and Only.
You shall love Hashem, your God, with all your heart, with all your
soul and with all of your resources. Let these matters that I command
you today be upon your heart. Teach them thoroughly to your chil-
dren and speak of them while you sit in your home, while you walk
on
the way, when you retire, and when you arise. Bind them as a sign
upon your arm and let them be tefillin between your eyes. And write
them on the doorposts of your house and upon your gates.
–Deuteronomy 6:5–9

This entire text is worthy of extensive study and conveys an abundance of insights that one could spend a lifetime delving into. We have selected a number of key phrases to convey the essence of the entire nature of the mezuzah and its relationship to how we can stay mindful of the spiritual potential within each place and each moment.

However, before we gather insights from the mezuzah scroll, we must ask ourselves two questions: "Why is it that we need such constant reminders about moving forward in our lives and being open to new possibilities for growth and change? Is there something that keeps us from moving forward?"

When we think about it, we'll remember that the holiday of Chanukah specifically focuses on the lesson of active trust. The miracles of Chanukah came through the ability to trust that God gives us everything we need to take the next step forward. Fear and lack of trust often keep us from moving forward. The mezuzah tells us, "Zooz! (Keep moving!)" The inside of the *mezuzah*—the words on the scroll—tells us how to do it.

"You shall love the Lord your God with all your heart, with all your soul, and with all your resources."

What does that mean? We are supposed to move forward and fulfill our purpose with everything we *do* have. We are not supposed to focus on, or concern ourselves with, what we don't have. This requires our heart and soul—an emotional and spiritual commitment, as well as the commitment of all our resources—whether material, intellectual, or financial. In other words, we need to give life our best and our all.

One reason we might be reluctant to give our best is that we often feel overwhelmed and overly concerned about what the outcome of our efforts might be. This kind of thinking can keep us stuck. But we do not have an obligation to control the results of our efforts. If our efforts are not successful, that may well be beyond our control. Fear of possible failure, then, is not a reason to refrain from putting in our best effort to do whatever we can. Fear of not having everything we need to move forward should not keep us from taking the initial steps necessary to begin. The results of our efforts are in God's hands.

A second obstacle that often comes up is that we don't know what we are moving toward. Moving forward assumes that we know what "forward" means. The holiday of Pesach teaches us about living with a vision of the future that illuminates our path and influences our choices in the present. Moving forward on a daily basis requires no less of a vision than the dramatic times of the exodus from Egypt.

God's vision for us, the Divine Design, is of a successfully unified spiritual and physical existence that brings us nourishment, satisfaction, and joy. This vision is what we crave as well. What gets in the way of our remembering this, and what prevents us from keeping this vision clearly in our minds, hearts, and souls?

What often interferes is what feels like the ordinariness of everyday life. We don't see the big picture of redemption unfolding as we do our grocery shopping, take our kids to the orthodontist, fold laundry, or work late at the office. The Torah's wisdom, inscribed on our mezuzah scroll, comes to tell us to use each and every one of those ordinary times to reinforce the message we are trying to remember. The command is:

"Teach them (the commandments) thoroughly to your children"
... and to yourselves too,

"...and speak of them while you sit in your home"
...at the dining room table, drying dishes in the
kitchen, playing games,

"while you walk on the way ..."
...driving to the mall, taking a road trip, going to work,

"when you retire ..."
...before you fall into bed after a long day,

"and when you arise ..."
...before your day gets ahead of you.

"Bind them as a sign upon your arm ..."
Make a physical reminder for yourself that will
make an impression on you,

"and let them be tefillin between your eyes ..."
keep it in your mind's eye always,

*"And write them on the doorposts of your house and upon your
gates."*
Remember that wherever you are and wherever
you are going, there is a spiritual
opportunity and doorway that awaits you.

This is how the message of the mezuzah can have a profound
effect and transform our everyday and seemingly ordinary lives
into extraordinary ones.

ALL UNDER ONE ROOF ...

A characteristic of daily life that can easily get in the way of maintaining a unified physical and spiritual vision is that our lives often seem not to have an underlying, unified structure. We tend to compartmentalize our lives—work, spouse, children, home, community activities, friends, appointments, and errands. Each aspect of life appears to be competing for our time, attention, and effort. However, just as each room of a house may have a very different function, we understand that the rooms are all under one roof and integrated into one household. Perhaps the opening line of the mezuzah, "Hear Israel, the Lord your God, the Lord is One," which affirms the absolute unity of God, can remind us that if all of reality has an underlying unity, then so do our lives.

Everything really is happening under one roof. Each room or aspect of our life has a specific purpose, but there are doorways that connect the rooms to create a home. Working to identify a guiding principle, mission, or vision for life will help us see and live our lives with a unified focus. Then we can understand how each part contributes to the whole. We can see that even when we are in the kitchen with its specific possibilities, we are also in our home with its overriding purpose. This is how having a mezuzah on every doorpost can remind us that while we are passing from one room to the next and one event to the next, there is always an underlying unity to guide us.

The mezuzah tells us to move, not in frenzy just for movement's sake, but forward with purpose, using every moment and every situation to connect with the Divine flow of life and to make our vision a reality. Our lives are too short and our potential too great to leave spiritual growth to chance. Many people have the custom of touching and kissing the mezuzah as they go in and out of their homes, and even as they move from room to room, to stay connected with God, the source of their unified vision, as they go about their day. The small mezuzah on every doorpost of our homes provides a quiet but constant reminder that time is moving and so should we. As we move through the hectic and seemingly disconnected days of our lives, our mezuzahs call our attention to, and give us the perspective of, the unified wholeness that does exist. This awareness can aid us in connecting and integrating all the different components of our daily lives. Taking a moment to kiss the mezuzah as we pass by it reminds us to recognize the opportunities for spiritual growth that await us at every moment and at every doorpost.

In this alcove of the mezuzah, we've seen that the words purposefully inscribed on the mezuzah parchment have a profound power to energize us. Words are potent.

The words we use to describe and define what we are experiencing at any given moment in time determine our attitudes, emotions, and actual responses to what we understand those words to mean. This phenomenon, to which we are oblivious for the most part, heavily impacts our spiritual growth. The words we choose to use in our self-talk, in which we engage nearly all of our waking moments, and the words we then use in conversation, are crucially important. Therefore, it is essential that we carefully and thoughtfully choose the words we use when we think or speak about our circumstances because the power of those words creates the reality in which we live.

We invite you now to come into the final room in our House of the Present. In this room, we will share six words that can change the way we look at and experience our lives. We call this room the Library of Our Mind.

VI.

The Library of
Our Mind

INTRODUCTION

LIKE ANY GRAND HOUSE, the House of the Present Moment has a library. This library, however, is unique. There are no books to be found in it. Instead, this library is filled with a collection of words. We dedicate this word library to words that shape our reality and help us live our lives more fully in the present. We call it The Library of Our Mind. The words that we're about to offer—the words and language we can use to describe, interpret, and direct our thoughts and actions—give us the most fundamental tools to be successful at living and thriving in the present moment.

"According to our sages, 'A person's mind follows his mouth.'"
—Chovos HaLevavos

Whether we realize it or not, each of us already has a library of the mind—a library filled with words, thoughts, and ideas that were chosen consciously, as well as collected unconsciously, that define our expectations and perceptions of the world and our responses to it. Think about it. People have philosophies of life that are often summed up in a few words or phrases, but that speak volumes about how they interpret what goes on around them. Just as we can learn about a person by looking at his or her home library and by seeing which books they check out from their local library, we can also learn a lot about a person by which words they "check out" from the library of their mind and use on a regular basis. When someone tells you, "It's a dog-eat-dog world out there," you can guess, unfortunately, what their actions might be when they are faced with a difficult ethical business decision. People who use phrases like, "Honesty is the best policy" probably have very different ways of living in the world than those who have, "Survival of the fittest" as their catchphrase.

Most regular libraries have professionals who choose which books and materials to put on the shelves. Unfortunately, the library of our mind usually is not handled as carefully. Most of us have never actively chosen which words we want in our library. While censorship in a regular library goes against our democratic sensibilities, it is very appropriate for our mental library.

CHOOSING DISCERNING WORDS ...

If we do not discern which words we put into our minds, we will find ourselves "checking out" words from the library of our mind that can lead us to false perceptions that cloud or distort our image of reality. We tend to live out the version of reality that our words describe, so it is counterproductive to our spiritual growth and sanity to be so "open-minded" and not be discriminating about which words fill our minds. When we let limiting words and ideas into our hearts and minds, we create a negative, frightening, and suffocating world for ourselves. We can stay stuck in the past in pain or fret about the future in fear.

Consciously choosing inspiring and encouraging words for our mental library can transform our reality and allow us to live more frequently and fully in the present moment. Words create our reality. When we read well-written fiction, we can believe and respond to what we are reading as if it were true. That's why we can read a very frightening suspense thriller and find ourselves with our hearts pounding and scared to death ... all while sitting safely curled up on our couch. Intellectually, we know that what we're reading isn't real, and yet we react as if it were.

The mind doesn't differentiate between what we imagine and what is real. The words we read trigger our imagination and create a reality that we respond to. We can cry, feel cold, be aroused, or laugh when we read. If that is the case with fiction, think how much more we can use words to shape our actual emotions, thoughts, and actions. We can use words to describe the memories of our past in a way that focuses on the wisdom we are striving to gain from the past. At the same time, when we use inspiring words to describe our vision for the future, those words will serve to guide us in the direction we hope to go. When we understand what words mean and the power they have, we can choose to create a nurturing reality that keeps us focused, strong, and in the present moment.

This library holds words of wisdom that can guide us in defining and creating our lives. It is time to browse, learn about, and choose the words that inspire you. You'll probably find words here that you'd like to have as your own, possibly exchanging them for some of the self-defeating words you've borrowed all too often from the library you already have. The library of the mind in the House of the Present Moment is always open. You can check out these new words whenever you wish, and you never need to return them.

ENTERING THE LIBRARY

As we enter the Library of our Mind, a cozy space with words of wisdom beautifully inscribed around the circumference of its softly illuminated walls embraces us. The library has a meditative feel to it, and it beckons us in to contemplate and think about why these words are here and what they have to teach us. Because these words have meanings and implications that are intertwined and connected, they flow in a circular path that draws us from one word to the next.

Having an entire vocabulary in our mind that we can attach to our perceptions and experiences strengthens our ability to stay focused in the present moment. We'll see the words we want to use to help bring and keep us in the present moment, and we'll look at the words we're probably using now that have kept us locked in the past or fearful of the future. We will recognize that the words of wisdom we encounter here are words that we already know; there's no complex vocabulary to learn. Until now, we might not have examined how powerful these words can be or recognized the shift in our outlook that they can create.

In this library, we are going to look at words that seem similar but which differ significantly when it comes to the thoughts, perceptions, and interpretations they stimulate. We'll look at both words—the one we may have been using and the one we may now want to adopt.

The first words we see are words that convey the level of trust we have while going about our daily lives, as well as the comfort we feel when making important decisions. These words address our concern for self-protection—a fundamental, reasonable, and necessary concern to have.

SAFETY VS. SECURITY

Most of us think we want to be safe. Who wouldn't? Safety means freedom from threat or harm of any kind. It means wanting nothing to come into our lives that might hurt us—be it burglars, germs, or bad news. We would really like, in some way, to be sealed in a bubble. Being safe is an intermittent state, temporary at best, and unattainable and illusory at worst. There's really no such thing as complete safety. No matter what we do, we can never achieve total safety. We can never be completely free from harm or risk. It is an impossible goal. Striving for safety can keep us locked in fear and anxiety, afraid to do or be something because we don't want to do anything that feels like a risk. Seeking safety inhibits us from moving forward and realizing the full potential of living in the present. In this case, we're not talking about taking normal precautions, such as wearing a seat belt while driving or a helmet while biking, or being careful walking alone in dark parking lots. What we are focusing on is looking at normal, everyday situations in the world as if they are overwhelming dangers.

WHERE DOES THIS COME FROM?

Seeking safety is a trap because it comes from a desire to control external situations and circumstances. The inability to control what will happen next causes worry, fear, and anxiety. Each and every moment we spend in worry, fear, or anxiety takes us out of the present moment and away from what truly is and could be unfolding right now.

If we can't have safety—physical, emotional, financial, etc.—what can we have? Let's look at a closely related, but very different word. Let's look at security.

SECURITY (w/ VIGILANCE) (AWARENESS) CAUTION FORSIGHT

Security is defined as freedom from the anxiety or apprehension of danger or risk. It is not freedom from the danger or risk itself. Security is the freedom from fear; it is having the confidence to move forward. Security is what we need to have to face the dangers and risks that we know are always there.

Think about a little child with her security blanket, toy, or thumb. Even the child knows that when we have security, we aren't expecting difficulties to go away; we just feel that we have support, and then we can muster the confidence and courage to face those difficulties. For a child, those challenges might be falling asleep in a dark room, being around strangers, or getting a shot. For us, as adults, it might be pursuing a dream that others ridicule, facing a difficult boss, or risking the pursuit of a new sport. Our fear of failure, pain, success, rejection, embarrassment, or loneliness requires giving up the desire for safety and looking instead for a source of security. Having a sense of security is something real that we can work on developing because it comes from the inside, without trying to control what's happening on the outside. Even with the external prop of a blanket, the child is really developing her internal ability to deal with life's challenges. Once she fully internalizes her sense of security, she will give up her blanket.

What is our source of security? What is our security blanket? If we remember the rooms we've been through in this House of the Present, we realize that many of the holidays, especially Sukkot, with its temporary and fragile structure, help to internalize the trust and sense of security that we can have in our lives. The double portion of challah that we have on Shabbat reaffirms our sense of financial security, while the maror on the seder plate reminds us that even when something painful does happen, we will be able to use the wisdom gained from it to move forward with trust and courage. We actually have a number of security blankets, and they are all reminders of our ultimate and real source of security—the Creator of the Universe who created us and whose guidance is constantly present. Realizing that God is our source of security helps to keep our concerns about safety within a normal range, so that we are not immobilized with fright. When we feel secure, our anxiety and apprehension diminish, and we can move forward with confidence and trust through the challenges that confront us and the opportunities that await us.

The desire to control everything so that we can feel safe is closely related to our belief that if something painful or difficult does happen, we will be defeated. The entire story of the exodus from Egypt and its centrality as the springboard to greater heights for us as individuals, as well as a people, reminds us that there is another word to use when we do, in fact, experience true hardships. That word is resilience and is a perfect substitute for defeat.

DEFEAT VS. RESILIENCE

The word defeat conjures up images of being deflated, de-terred, and dejected. To feel defeated means to feel frustrated, destroyed, overthrown, or resigned. The sense of finality in this word stops us from going anywhere. When we use and live the word "defeated," we are assuming that the current situation is a permanent state and that nothing good can come from our situation because nothing will ever change. This perspective creates an attitude that trips up many people in their journey through life. It is similar to the word safety, which is focused on the impossible goal of controlling external situations and circumstances. In this case, one feels defeat when they believe outside influences are controlling their state of being and that those influences are static or permanent. There is another word that helps a person mobilize internal and external resources to respond to difficulties, using both the wisdom gained from the painful situation as well as a vision of improved circumstances. That word is "resilience."

RESILIENCE

The word resilience sounds like brilliance, and rolls off the tongue in a wave of motion. Resilience means the ability to recover or adjust easily to misfortune or change. It means the ability to withstand shock without permanent deformation or rupture. It means to bounce back. Obviously, a situation that has caused stress or strain precedes the need for resilience. In life circumstances, resilience is what we need when we're tempted to perceive defeat. We could cultivate resilience through exciting experiences that test our endurance, but one doesn't need to live a life of high adventure to develop resilience in the face of challenges. Resilience is required only when difficult, painful, or unpleasant things happen. Resilience requires recognizing that the pain or negative energy that a difficulty creates is still energy that can be harnessed. Taking control of that energy, and combining it with the power of memory to access wisdom plus the power of imagination to visualize positive steps we can take, enables us to regain our equilibrium. By channeling and transforming the negative energy, we have the ability to propel ourselves forward ... in other words, to be resilient.

Some people's stories of resilience are nearly unbelievable. In our generation, Jewish people refer to the Holocaust when thinking about the worst things that can happen to a person. Returning to the story about Viktor Frankl, which we mentioned near the beginning of the book, we see an inspiring example of resilience. Dr. Frankl, author of *Man's Search for Meaning* and a leading psychiatrist, endured years of torture in a Nazi concentration camp. Unable to change his circumstances, he made the conscious decision to harness the tremendous negativity of his situation and focus on what he could control—his attitude and response to what his captors and tormentors tried to do to him. Dr. Frankl made the decision to use his horrific concentration camp experiences, as he suffered through them, as lessons for learning about human potential and behavior. He neither denied the pain of his experiences nor dwelt on his suffering; rather, he used the gifts of memory and imagination to learn and grow. He chose to cultivate resilience rather than letting his captors defeat him. God willing, none of us will ever get called upon to be this resilient. However, we all suffer big and small setbacks throughout our lives. Recognizing and remembering our potential for resilience, rather than defeat, will go a long way in enabling us to grow from everything that happens to us.

The entire process of teshuvah (return) is one of resilience, as is the story of the exodus from Egypt. Teshuvah teaches us that we can turn around poor choices in life. We don't have to be defeated by our falls along the way. The pain of our bondage in Egypt became the springboard for our resilience as a people. Resilience recognizes that life's journey can always be in a state of flow and that we are moving and growing, even when we are being nourished with bitter waters. We want to be like a flowing stream that continues on its way even when boulders, trees, or other debris attempts to block it. Water may be detoured, but it is not deterred. A flowing stream is an expression of resilience and reminds us of our true potential.

When we activate our resilience, we activate the ability to be responsive rather than reactive. These are the next two words, which many people use interchangeably, but which, in reality, are very different.

REACTIVE VS. RESPONSIVE

To react means to act again. It is a word used in the world of science to describe predictable relationships between chemicals. When it comes to chemical reactions, we are relying on that predictability. We want two chemicals to react the same way every time we put them together. However, real life is not a chemistry lab, and while reacting works well for chemicals, in real-life situations, a reactive approach is antithetical to living in the present moment. Being reactive means that in any given situation, we act the same way we always have in the past, whether it's appropriate to the current situation or not. People often use the metaphor of "replaying old tapes" when they refer to situations that trigger an automatic, reflexive reaction. Reactions cause us to be oblivious to new information or other subtle differences and opportunities that exist. This happens because we tend to be attuned to and only perceive messages and input that seem familiar or the same as they were in the past. Therefore, we react the way we have in the past. What makes that way of thinking and being so deadening is that it almost guarantees that we will replay and re-experience a situation the same as we always have. The truth is, no situation is ever exactly the same as it was before. Being reactive means we ignore this truth and live in an artificial reality. There is another approach and a better word: responsive.

RESPONSIVE

Responsive means to respond or to answer. Answering implies hearing or recognizing what someone is communicating and what is happening—not what we think is or have predicted would be happening based on the past. When responsive, we are in a form of dialogue with reality. Responsiveness means paying attention and being open to the new potential and possibilities that are in every moment. This doesn't mean that we abandon our common sense. If we find ourselves in a conversation or a situation with someone who was harmful to us in the past, it is important to recognize a need for caution, but we don't need to come out swinging before anything has been said or done. Our example of Miriam's response to Pharaoh's daughter holding Moses is a great model for us to use. Miriam's reaction could have been one of panic—*Pharaoh's daughter has my brother*. Instead, Miriam waited and read the situation for what it really was, rather than assuming that it was a terrible occurrence. She saw that Pharaoh's daughter was going to protect Moses, and Miriam responded to her with the appropriate question: "Shall I go and summon for you a wet nurse from the Hebrew women, who will nurse the boy for you?" (Exodus 1:7). Her desire to live in the present and be responsive, rather than reactive, caused a pivotal event in Moses's life and in the lives and history of the Jewish people.

Being responsive means checking out another word from our Library of the Mind. That word is poised, rather than its counterpart that many of us display all too often: paralyzed. Let's understand the difference between the two.

PARALYZED VS. POISED

Mental paralysis means not having the ability to move one's thoughts forward, and it causes a state of powerlessness and incapacity to act. When someone is paralyzed with fear, doubt, or uncertainty, their inability to make choices in the present moment severely handicaps them. Often, before anything at all even happens, the fearful person is already paralyzed. We can begin to see a pattern here: a person who is always seeking safety lives in a world of fear. If anything does happen to that person, he experiences his pain and suffering as defeat. When faced with anything like it in the future, he either reacts in fear or is paralyzed. Someone who is paralyzed doesn't move because they can't. However, all stillness is not paralysis. There is another word—poised—which also conveys stillness, but the lack of movement it conveys is for very different reasons.

POISED

When we say that someone is poised, we usually think of someone who has an inner-centeredness. They are unflappable and seem to carry themselves with an internal equilibrium. Like security, resilience, and responsiveness, poise is a state of being that comes from the inside and is not dependent on external circumstances. Poised also means to be still, to weigh, to ponder, and to have readiness. A tiger that is poised in the bushes awaiting its prey is not still because of paralysis. It is still because it is waiting expectantly. Again, Miriam, at the water's edge after sending Moses down the Nile in a basket, was poised, waiting to see what would happen, ready to respond at the first opportunity. The tiger and Miriam have something in common: they both waited for something to happen that would further their goal. The tiger awaits food and is ready to spring into action as soon as prey comes its way. Miriam awaited redemption and anything that looked like it could help deliverance unfold—however subtle the step or opportunity might be—would make her spring into action as well. When we live our lives poised, we will be ready for opportunities that come, trusting that they are specifically for us.

When we strive to be poised rather than feel paralyzed, we are able to act: we can prepare rather than predict. These two words also seem similar, but the results from one are very different than the other.

PREDICT VS. PREPARE

To predict literally means to *pre-say* or to declare in advance. We love predictions. Predictions give us a feeling of control; we think we know what is going to happen. That's why people consult astrology charts, tarot cards, and tea leaves. The desire to be omniscient is very strong. However, focusing on predictions, like focusing on safety, is self-defeating because it is not based on reality. The truth is there is very little we can predict because most situations are comprised of many and complex variables that interact with each other in unpredictable ways. Given human limitations, we can be aware of only a few of these variables, no matter how clairvoyant we think we are. When we try to predict something—be it failure, success, or anything else—we take ourselves out of the realm of being responsive to what is unfolding before us.

With time and imagination, it is easy to become invested in our predictions. We will find ourselves constantly looking for evidence that our predictions are coming true. When we live with predictions like, "I'll never be good at tennis, math, or gardening," we set ourselves up for failure. We won't attempt to pursue our dreams of what we'd really love to become or do. We will interpret each and every setback that comes along as verification of our negative prediction. There is something in human nature that often makes us prefer being correct to being happy. We feel powerful and in control when we can say, "I knew it," or "I told you so." Making predictions, especially negative ones, takes us out of the House of the Present.

God gave human beings the incredible gift of imagination. Rather than using it to conjure up dire predictions, we have another approach, associated with a word that also requires imagination, but which directs us and allows us to be positive and action-oriented. The word we want to examine from the Library of Our Mind is: prepare.

PREPARE

To prepare means to make ready, to arrange, to make suitable beforehand, and to equip. Prepare is certainly a future-focused word and requires us to assess our current situation or circumstance honestly and have a vision of what we would like to accomplish. It is productive to acknowledge that there is a gap between our current state and where we hope to be. It is fine to say, "I'm not good at gardening, tennis, or math," if that's the reality at the moment. If we don't have an accurate view of our present situation, we will handicap ourselves because we won't be able to recognize what needs to change.

When we focus on preparations rather than predictions, however, we stay in the House of the Present Moment because that focus encourages us to ask the question, for example, "What can I do right now to prepare myself for becoming a better tennis player?" Asking this kind of question opens up many possibilities: "I can sign up for tennis lessons, or I can ask my friend to play with me and give me some pointers." When I ask how I can prepare for the future, I can see that there are often many possibilities, and I become empowered to take action. Even when it isn't possible to take physical action, it is always possible to make mental and emotional preparations. Successful Olympic athletes will tell you that when they are not able to practice physically, they spend time visualizing their skating routines, ski courses, or swimming strokes. Talking, thinking, meditating, collecting information, and planning are all examples of making preparations for whatever it is we would like to achieve. Focusing on preparations, rather than on predictions, gives us a way to use our imagination and "future-thinking" to flourish in the present moment. The very act of focusing on preparations diminishes the heaviness of fear that often overwhelms and immobilizes us when we wallow in "prediction-making." Preparations transform the energy of fear into the energy of positive action.

When we consciously choose the word "prepare" rather than "predict," we can manage, not control, what happens to us. These two words—manage and control—are the final word set we want to look at. They help determine how we experience what happens in our lives.

CONTROL VS. MANAGE

Control means to restrain, to have power over, or to determine an outcome. Once we understand the definition of this word, we can see that the desire to have control, like the desire to have total safety, is wishful thinking and impossible. Can we begin to understand how frustrating and difficult our lives will seem to be if these are the criteria we have for being successful and happy? While it is a worthwhile goal to learn self-control because that is in the realm of possibility and responsibility, unfortunately, that sort of control is usually not our focus. We want to control other people, the traffic, our bosses, the weather, and world politics. We get frustrated because it makes our sense of well-being dependent on what other people are doing and what other factors are at play. Wanting to be in control takes us out of the House of the Present Moment because neither our wisdom nor our imagination is sufficient or useful to put us in control. What are we supposed to do? When we substitute the word "manage" for "control," we open up to realistic possibilities in the present moment.

MANAGE

To manage means to direct or carry on affairs, and to handle. The word manage comes from the Latin *mano*, meaning hand. To manage means to focus on what is *in* our hands to do, rather than on what is *out* of our hands. The saying, "We cannot control the wind, but we can set our sails," summarizes this idea. A business manager cannot control the economy but can respond to changing circumstances. Miriam could not control Pharaoh's edicts, but she could encourage the women to continue having children in spite of his harsh decrees. The Maccabees who led the revolt that resulted in the holiday of Chanukah couldn't control the Syrian-Greeks who wanted to destroy Judaism, but they could band together to fight with what they had—faith, courage, and a handful of devoted people.

There is always something that is in our hands to do. Being a good life manager means being in the flow of the moment, responsive to what is happening, and using whatever is at hand to handle the situation. Managing means living fully in the House of the Present Moment because it takes wisdom gained from the past, as well as a vision of the future, to negotiate and navigate life's journey. A person who seeks to be in control is pained, angry, and frustrated when things don't go as expected or predicted; a person who strives to manage is proud and satisfied when he can carry on and respond to unexpected or difficult circumstances.

If we look at a composite picture of a person who lives by the first set of words from our library (safety, defeat, reactive, paralyzed, prediction, control) compared to a person who lives by the second set of words (security, resilience, responsive, poised, preparation, manage), we see two very different people leading two very different lives. The first set of words all have something in common: they are focused externally. People who feel defined by these words are always in survival mode because they believe they are at the mercy of circumstances outside of themselves. Their lives can be miserable and a constant struggle.

On the other hand, people who learn to cultivate a sense of security realize they can be resilient, respond to new circumstances as they unfold, and are poised to live a rewarding life. The attitudes these words represent are determined internally. People who live by those words feel empowered to prepare in whatever way they can and will manage whatever comes their way with the wisdom and vision they have access to by living in the present moment. These people are centered internally and can maintain or regain their equilibrium. Challenges and difficulties don't capsize them. Their trust and faith enable them to harness the wisdom gained from their experiences and to hold their vision's beacon of light for the future as they move forward on life's journey. Their goal is to thrive, rather than merely to survive, and they can find serenity even in the most difficult circumstances.

A person whose goal in life is only to survive misses the opportunity to reach his or her full potential in this world. To thrive, which means to grow vigorously, flourish, prosper, and progress toward a goal, is the assignment our souls were given when they came into this world. Simple survival is the goal of the animal kingdom. Animals are programmed with a survival instinct. They are not given the resources or the inclination to become wholly fulfilled. A cow cannot decide that eating grass is a thing of the past and that it now wants to go to culinary school to explore different options. Striving toward a goal is for human beings. Human beings also have a survival instinct, but that is at the lowest level of human existence and certainly doesn't represent what a human being is all about. If we are just in this world to survive, we would have no need for a soul. The fact that we have a soul tells us that there must be something more for us to do and to become in this world. To thrive, body and soul is only possible when we live in the present moment and make use of all of the gifts that God has given us.

Because we have free will, we could choose to use our memory of the past to keep us locked in pain and our imagination of the future to keep us paralyzed in fear. The dramatic choice we have is that we can either make our lives meaningless or magnificent. Choosing words that cultivate a way of being in the world is part of the choice we make.

Our tradition teaches that God created the world using words. So, too, we create our world using words. Imagine the life we would create if we checked out and used only the positive words from the Library of Our Mind to make our life a true bestseller.

VII.

This House is Now Yours

THE KEYS ARE IN YOUR HANDS

AS OUR TOUR OF THE HOUSE of the Present Moment comes to a close, let's return to Miriam's Courtyard, where we can spend a few moments reflecting on this distinctive house that we have explored, with all its different rooms and alcoves.

As soon as we entered the House of the Present Moment, we could sense that we were in a special place. We came into this beautifully landscaped courtyard with its fountain and benches, and we felt refreshed by our surroundings. The courtyard introduced us to Miriam's life and her ability to thrive in the flow of the living moment. She lived her life being able to bring the wisdom from the past and an inspiring vision of the future to each moment she experienced and every decision she made. The stories about her approach and response to the challenging events in her life were inspiring, but we wanted to find out how we could develop her same qualities in ourselves.

This question led us to continue our tour inside the House of the Present to discover how the Divine Design is specifically structured to help us practice and strengthen the skills and qualities we need to live in the present moment. As we explored each of the rooms and alcoves of the house, we expanded our understanding of how each space contributed something different. We saw that the Shabbat, Holiday, Passover, and Mitzvot Rooms each encompass and express unique elements of the Divine Design. We saw that each room gives ongoing, varied opportunities to enhance our ability to live in the present moment. The last room we visited was the Library of Our Mind, where we were able to identify key words that can guide us in choosing attitudes, beliefs, and perspectives to help us live with internal focus and serenity.

We hope you have been inspired by what you have experienced on this tour. It might not be obvious, though, how to begin applying the inspiration you've gained to your daily life. How do you turn your inspiration into action? How do you begin to build your personal House of the Present Moment? The truth is that you don't need to start from the beginning and try to build from the ground up. This House of the Present Moment that we have toured actually already belongs to you. It is your inheritance. You can take ownership of it right now, move in, and begin living here. And you never need to move out of it. As described at the beginning of the book, the Divine Design, with which the House of the Present Moment was constructed, is based on the ancient and deep wisdom of Torah and Judaism. You are the rightful owner of this wisdom. It has been given to you to help you live in the present moment and to fulfill your potential in a joyful and meaningful way.

We invite you to go back now and take another look at the wisdom and guiding light of each room. Choose a place that feels comfortable to begin. Make yourself at home. Each room offers you tremendous opportunities for personal growth.

Because there is an underlying unity and spiritual current that runs throughout this house, it doesn't matter where you begin. Each of the rooms flows into the next; you can begin wherever you feel the strongest, or perhaps the most comfortable, personal connection. It will help to start with something small. Pick one alcove or even one word, and let it grow on you and with you. Implementing small changes based on the Divine Design can have a big impact on helping you live in the present moment. You are the master of this home. It is your mind and heart and soul that will be affected to the extent that you integrate the ideas we've shared within these pages. Although we have reached the conclusion of our tour, the pleasure of living your life here in the House of the Present Moment has just begun.

IDEAS TO GET YOU STARTED ...

To get started, we suggest you try one or more of the ideas that follow, to help the Divine Design begin to express itself in your life.

- You may initially want to go back to the Library of Our Mind and choose one word that resonates with you, to become your own personal watchword or *mantra*, having it be in your mind and on your lips as you go throughout your day. That word can be a key to begin opening up opportunities for further growth and transformation. See what happens when you become mindful of a word that focuses your attention in a positive direction and which can encapsulate your goal.

- Think about a challenge or a situation you are currently facing and choose one of the rooms or alcoves that focuses on a particular idea that is relevant to something you are experiencing now in your life. You can refer back to the table of contents which will remind you about the major themes of each alcove, so you can select the best place to begin.

- In anticipation of one of the Jewish holidays, select one of the rooms or alcoves to heighten your enjoyment of that holiday and draw more inspiration for your celebration of it, while at the same time becoming motivated to internalize and apply its profound messages.

- After celebrating a holiday that is described in this book, select the room or the alcove that is connected to that holiday to prolong and deepen the lessons learned from it, as you actively use those lessons in your life situations and challenges.

- Choose an alcove from the Mizvot Room for a mitzvah you're already doing and re-connect to and embrace the message it has for you regarding living more expansively in the present moment.

- If you feel adventuresome, try a mitzvah that's new to you and use the insights conveyed in the alcove related to that mitzvah to make it meaningful to you and to impact your desire for spiritual connection and personal growth.

THE KEYS ARE IN YOUR HANDS.
WELCOME HOME!

We hope you will find joy and fulfillment living in the House of the Present Moment and that your life will be enriched by the Divine Design that creates it. Please feel free to let us know which ideas are most useful to you and how you are using them.

You can reach us at: livinginthepresent.book@gmail.com.

Ellyn & Teena

VIII.

Glossary

GLOSSARY AND
MONTHS OF THE YEAR

GLOSSARY

Afikoman—Piece of matza hidden at the beginning of the Passover Seder and eaten at the end of the Seder which serves as "dessert."

Brit Milah or Bris—Covenant of circumcision performed on the eighth day after a baby boy is born.

Challah—Special bread eaten on Shabbat and holidays, often braided.

Chametz—All foods prohibited during Passover, including leavened bread.

Chanukah—Festival celebrating the miracle of the tiny Jewish army over the Syrian Greeks and the miracle of the oil for the Menorah meant to last one day but which lasted eight days.

Charoset—Sweet mixture of apples, wine, and nuts (or other sweet ingredients) that the maror is dipped into at the Passover seder.

Elul—Month on the Hebrew calendar that is designated for spiritual preparations for the high holidays.

Haggada—Special book used to guide the Passover Seder containing all the readings, blessings, and stories.

Havdalah—Ceremony marking the end of Shabbat and separating it from the six days of the regular week.

Kohen/Kohanim—Aaron (Moshe's brother) and his descendants who make up the priestly class of the Jewish people.

Maccabees—The Jewish warriors who led the Jewish people to victory against the Syrian-Greek army (Chanukah).

Manna—The heavenly food that fell each day, was gathered, and sustained the Jewish people during the forty years in the Midbar (desert) after leaving Egypt.

Maror—The bitter herbs (horseradish or romaine lettuce) eaten at the Passover Seder.

Matza—Unleavened bread eaten during Passover.

Mayim—Water.

Menorah/Chanukiah—The special eight-branched candelabra that is lit each night of Chanukah.

Mezuzah—Scroll containing excerpts from the Torah that is placed in a cylindrical or rectangular container and placed on each doorway throughout the home.

Midbar—Desert or wilderness that the Jewish people lived in for forty years after the exodus from Egypt and before entering the Land of Israel.

Mikveh—A naturally collected body of water used for immersion and spiritual transformation.

Mitzrayim—Egypt, literally "narrow."

Mitzvah/mitzvot—Points of connection we are commanded to either perform or refrain from in order to connect to God, actualize our potential, and stay safe.

Neshama—Soul.

Netilat Yadayim—Literally to elevate the hands, but used in reference to the ritual handwashing, which spiritually elevates the use of our hands.

Passover/Pesach—The holiday celebrating our liberation from Egyptian bondage and the freedom to serve God.

Rosh Chodesh—Literally the "new head" but meant to refer to the new month or the new moon.

Rosh Hashanah—The New Year (literally head of the year) and the Day of Judgment.

Seder—Literally means "order." Seder is the name of the interactive service done primarily in the home on the first night of Passover (or the first and second night of Passover for those living outside the Land of Israel).

Shamash—The "helper" candle used to light the Chanukah candles, but which does not count as one of the eight candles lit.

Shechinah—The Divine Presence of God, which is experienced as imminent rather than transcendent. The Shechinah is often considered the feminine aspect of God.

Siddur—Prayer book used for daily and for Shabbat prayer. The word "siddur" is related to the word "seder," which means "order" and refers to the order of prayers contained within it.

Shofar—Ram's horn blown on Rosh Hashana and Yom Kippur, as well as every day except Shabbat during the month of Elul.

Sukkah—Temporary structure or booth that we're commanded to build and spend time in (eating, drinking, sleeping, and visiting) for seven days during the holiday of Sukkot.

Sukkot—The seven-day holiday celebrating the Divine Presence being close to us and giving us spiritual security.

Tefillin—Black boxes containing specific verses written on parchment worn on a man's forehead and upper, inner arm.

Teshuvah—— Frequently translated as "repentance," but more accurately meaning "return to our true self."

Tzedaka—Justice or righteousness, but often translated as "charity" when the word is used in reference to money.

Yom Kippur—The Day of Atonement when sins are forgiven.

Zooz—Command form: "Move!"

HEBREW MONTHS OF THE YEAR

The Hebrew calendar, being primarily lunar, does not completely correspond to the exact English months each year. This listing notes the approximate correlation. While the Jewish year changes in Tishrei/Rosh Hashanah, the months are on a different cycle, which begins with Nisan in the spring. This is the order we have included for you here along with the holidays that occur in each month:

Nisan—Passover (April): God's Love and the Miracle of Redemption

Iyar—Lag B'Omer (May): Making the Effort to Grow Day-by-Day

Sivan—Shavuot (June): Receiving the Torah

Tammuz—Seventeenth of Tammuz (July): Cultivating a "Good Eye" and Seeing the Positive in Others

Av—Tisha b'Av and Tu b'Av (August): Working on Our Interpersonal Relationships

Elul—Preparation for the holidays in Tishrei (September): Taking Stock of Ourselves

Tishrei—Rosh Hashanah, Yom Kippur, Sukkot, Shemini Atzeret, and Simchat Torah (High Holidays) (October): Celebrating Our Ability to Change and Return to Purity

Cheshvan—No holidays (November): Putting the Results of our Spiritual Efforts During Tishrei into Effect

Kislev—Chanukah (December Dedication and Education, Moving Forward with What We Have

Tevet—Chanukah, Tenth of Tevet (January): Keeping the Spiritual Light in Times of Darkness

Shevat—Tu B'Shevat (February): Trusting in Our Potential for Growth

Adar – Purim (March): Seeing Miracles in the Ordinary Events of Our Lives

IX.

Appendix
of Blessings

APPENDIX OF BLESSINGS

Being mindful of what we are doing or experiencing isn't easy. When we pause and verbalize what we want to focus on, there is a better chance we will be present to and benefit from what we are doing. As we went through each of the rooms in the House of the Present Moment, we explored a number of rituals. Many of those rituals are connected to specific blessings we say before we do them. People seek and appreciate spirituality. We think it is helpful to know that the word "ritual" is in the word "spiritual." In Judaism, we use blessings to help us create a state of connection between our hearts, minds, and actions and the spiritual ideal we are striving to reach and integrate. Below is a collection of the blessings said for the various holidays and rituals that we presented throughout the book. Please feel free to consult a complete siddur (prayer book) for additional information and guidance in how and when to say each blessing. Each blessing appears in Hebrew, transliteration, and translation so you can use whichever form is most comfortable for you.

This section contains the holy Name of God written in Hebrew and therefore should be treated respectfully. Please take to your local synagogue should you choose to part with this book.

SHABBAT CANDLE LIGHTING

The lighting of candles as sunset approaches on Friday is the traditional sign of the arrival of Shabbat. After lighting the candles, it is customary to cover your eyes and say the following:

בָּרוּךְ אַתָּה ה' אֱלֹקֵינוּ מֶלֶךְ הָעוֹלָם אֲשֶׁר קִדְּשָׁנוּ בְּמִצְוֹתָיו
וְצִוָּנוּ לְהַדְלִיק נֵר שֶׁל שַׁבָּת

Baruch ata Adonai, Eloheinu Melech ha-olam, asher kidshanu b'mitzvotav vitzivanu l'hadlik ner shel Shabbat.

Blessed are You, God, Crowned Sovereign of the universe, Who sanctified us with the commandments and commanded us to light Shabbat candles.

KIDDUSH - BLESSING OVER WINE OR GRAPE JUICE ON FRIDAY NIGHT:

Some people recite just the regular blessing over wine before the Friday night meal.

בָּרוּךְ אַתָּה ה' אֱלֹקֵינוּ מֶלֶךְ הָעוֹלָם בּוֹרֵא פְּרִי הַגָּפֶן

Baruch ata Adonai, Eloheinu Melech ha-olam, boreh p'ri hagafen

Blessed are You, God, Crowned Sovereign of the universe, Who creates the fruit of the vine.

וַיְהִי עֶרֶב וַיְהִי בֹקֶר

יוֹם הַשִּׁשִּׁי. וַיְכֻלּוּ הַשָּׁמַיִם וְהָאָרֶץ וְכָל צְבָאָם

וַיְכַל אֱלֹקִים בַּיּוֹם הַשְּׁבִיעִי מְלַאכְתּוֹ אֲשֶׁר עָשָׂה. וַיִּשְׁבֹּת בַּיּוֹם הַשְּׁבִיעִי מִכָּל מְלַאכְתּוֹ אֲשֶׁר עָשָׂה

וַיְבָרֶךְ אֱלֹקִים אֶת יוֹם הַשְּׁבִיעִי וַיְקַדֵּשׁ אֹתוֹ. כִּי בוֹ שָׁבַת מִכָּל מְלַאכְתּוֹ אֲשֶׁר בָּרָא אֱלֹקִים לַעֲשׂוֹת

סַבְרִי מָרָנָן וְרַבָּנָן וְרַבּוֹתַי

בָּרוּךְ אַתָּה ה' אֱלֹקֵינוּ מֶלֶךְ הָעוֹלָם בּוֹרֵא פְּרִי הַגָּפֶן

בָּרוּךְ אַתָּה ה' אֱלֹקֵינוּ מֶלֶךְ הָעוֹלָם. אֲשֶׁר קִדְּשָׁנוּ בְּמִצְוֹתָיו וְרָצָה בָנוּ. וְשַׁבַּת קָדְשׁוֹ בְּאַהֲבָה וּבְרָצוֹן הִנְחִילָנוּ. זִכָּרוֹן לְמַעֲשֵׂה בְרֵאשִׁית. כִּי הוּא יוֹם תְּחִלָּה לְמִקְרָאֵי קֹדֶשׁ זֵכֶר לִיצִיאַת מִצְרָיִם. כִּי בָנוּ בָחַרְתָּ וְאוֹתָנוּ קִדַּשְׁתָּ מִכָּל הָעַמִּים וְשַׁבַּת קָדְשְׁךָ בְּאַהֲבָה וּבְרָצוֹן הִנְחַלְתָּנוּ

בָּרוּךְ אַתָּה ה' מְקַדֵּשׁ הַשַּׁבָּת

(Quietly: Va-y'hee erev, va-y'hee boker.)
Yom ha-shishi. Vay'chulu hashamayim v'ha-aretz v'chol tz'va'am.
Vay'chal Elohim bayom hash'vi'i milachto asher asa. Vayishbot bayom
hash'vi'i mikol milachto asher asa. Vay'varech Elohim et yom hash'vi'i
vay'kadesh oto. Kee vo shabbat mi-kol m'lachto asher bara Elohim
la'asot.

Savri maranan v'rabanan v'rabotai. Baruch ata Adonai, Eloheinu
melech ha-olam, borei p'ri hagafen.

Baruch ata Adonai, Eloheinu melech ha-olam, asher kid'shanu
b'mitzvotav v'ratza vanu, v'shabbat kod'sho b'ahava uv'ratzon
hinchilanu, zikaron l'ma'aseh b'reishit. Ki hu yom t'chila l'mikra-ay
kodesh, zaycher l'tziat mitzrayim. Ki vanu vacharta v'otanu kidashta
mikol ha'amim. V'shabbat kod-shi-cha b'ahava uv'ratzon hinchal
tanu. Baruch ata Adonai, mi'kadesh ha Shabbat.

Praise to You, Lord our God, Crowned Sovereign of the universe,
Creator of the fruit of the vine.

Praise to You, Lord our God, Crowned Sovereign of the universe
who finding favor with us, sanctified us with mitzvot.
In love and favor, You made the holy Shabbat our heritage
as a reminder of the work of Creation.
As first among our sacred days, it recalls the Exodus from Egypt
You chose us and set us apart from the peoples.
In love and favor You have given us Your holy Shabbat as an
inheritance.
Praise to You, God, who sanctifies Shabbat.

BLESSING OVER HAND WASHING (N'TILAT YADAYIM)

The same blessing is said in the morning when arising and washing hands.

Following Kiddush, it is customary to wash one's hands prior to making the blessing over the Challah and continuing the meal. After washing the hands with water from a cup—often twice on the right hand and twice on the left, though precise practices vary—the following blessing is recited:

בָּרוּךְ אַתָּה ה' אֱלֹקֵינוּ מֶלֶךְ הָעוֹלָם אֲשֶׁר קִדְּשָׁנוּ בְּמִצְוֹתָיו
וְצִוָּנוּ עַל נְטִילַת יָדַיִם

Baruch ata Adonai, Eloheinu Melech ha-olam, asher kidshanu b'mitzvotav vitzivanu al n'tilat yadayim.

Blessed are You, Lord our God, Crowned Sovereign of the universe, Who has sanctified us with His commandments, and commanded us concerning the washing of the hands.

BLESSING OVER THE BREAD (HAMOTZI)

After the washing of hands, we have the custom of remaining silent until after the blessing is made and the bread is eaten. This is to create a connection and focus our attention on what we are about to do. Prior to eating the bread, the following blessing is recited:

בָּרוּךְ אַתָּה ה' אֱלֹקֵינוּ מֶלֶךְ הָעוֹלָם הַמוֹצִיא לֶחֶם מִן הָאָרֶץ

Baruch ata Adonai, Eloheinu Melech ha-olam, hamotzi lechem min ha'aretz.

Blessed are You, Lord our God, Crowned Sovereign of the universe, Who brings forth bread from the earth.

HAVDALAH BLESSINGS

When Shabbat is over, we mark its passing and welcome the new week. The blessings over wine or grape juice, spices, and the light of a flame, along with a blessing that recognizes the important distinctions we make in our life, make up the Havdalah ceremony. Havdalah is introduced with the following prayer and then the individual blessings are said.

INTRODUCTORY READING

Many people begin with this introductory paragraph:

הִנֵּה אֵל יְשׁוּעָתִי, אֶבְטַח וְלֹא אֶפְחָד, כִּי עָזִּי וְזִמְרָת קָהּ ה'
וַיְהִי לִי לִישׁוּעָה. וּשְׁאַבְתֶּם מַיִם בְּשָׂשׂוֹן, מִמַּעַיְנֵי הַיְשׁוּעָה.
לַה' הַיְשׁוּעָה, עַל עַמְּךָ בִרְכָתֶךָ סֶּלָה. ה' צְבָאוֹת עִמָּנוּ, מִשְׂגָּב
לָנוּ אֱלֹהֵי יַעֲקֹב סֶלָה. ה' צְבָאוֹת, אַשְׁרֵי אָדָם בֹּטֵחַ בָּךְ. ה'
הוֹשִׁיעָה, הַמֶּלֶךְ יַעֲנֵנוּ בְיוֹם קָרְאֵנוּ. לַיְהוּדִים הָיְתָה אוֹרָה וְשִׂ-
מְחָה וְשָׂשׂוֹן וִיקָר. כֵּן תִּהְיֶה לָנוּ. כּוֹס יְשׁוּעוֹת אֶשָּׂא, וּבְשֵׁם
ה' אֶקְרָא

Hinei El yeshuati, evtach velo efchad, ki ozi vezimrat yah, Adonai vayehili liyeshuah. Ushavtem mayim besasson mima'anei hayeshuah. La'Adonai hayeshuah, al amcha virchatecha, selah. Adonai tzeva'ot imanu, misgav lanu, Elohay Ya'akov, selah. Adonai tzeva'ot, ashray adam botayach bach. Adonai hoshi'ah, hamelech ya'anaynu veyom koraynu. Layehudim hayetah orah vesimcha vesason vikar. Kain tehi-yeh lanu. Kos yeshuot esa uveshaym Adonai ekrah.

Behold, God is my Savior, I will trust God and not be afraid, for my strong faith and song of praise for God will be my salvation. You will draw water joyously from the wellsprings of salvation. Salvation is God's. May Your blessing rest upon Your people. God of the heavenly armies is with us; the Lord of Jacob is a fortress protecting us. God of the heavenly armies, happy is the individual who trusts You. God, redeem us! The King will answer us on the day we call God. The Jews had light, happiness, joy and honor; may we have the same. I will raise the cup of salvation and call out in the name of the God.

THE BLESSING OVER WINE
OR GRAPE JUICE

בָּרוּךְ אַתָּה ה' אֱלֹקֵינוּ מֶלֶךְ הָעוֹלָם, בּוֹרֵא פְּרִי הַגָּפֶן

Baruch atah, Adonai, Elohaynu melech ha'olam, boray pri hagafen.

Blessed are You, God, our Lord, Crowned Sovereign of the universe, Creator of the fruit of the vine. (We wait to drink the wine until the entire Havdalah ceremony has concluded.)

The blessing over spices

בָּרוּךְ אַתָּה ה' אֱלֹקֵינוּ מֶלֶךְ הָעוֹלָם, בּוֹרֵא מִינֵי בְשָׂמִים

Baruch atah, Adonai, Elohaynu melech ha'olam, boray minay besa-mim.

Blessed are You, God, our Lord, King of the universe, Creator of the different spices. (Smell the spices)

The blessing over the candle

בָּרוּךְ אַתָּה ה' אֱלֹקֵינוּ מֶלֶךְ הָעוֹלָם, בּוֹרֵא מְאוֹרֵי הָאֵשׁ

Baruch atah, Adonai, Elohaynu melech ha'olam, boray me'oray ha'aysh.

Blessed are You, God, our Lord, Crowned Sovereign of the universe, Creator of the fire's lights. (Hold fingers close to the flames and look at the shadow they cast.)

The blessing over havdalah

בָּרוּךְ אַתָּה ה' אֱלֹקֵינוּ מֶלֶךְ הָעוֹלָם, הַמַּבְדִּיל בֵּין קֹדֶשׁ לְחוֹל,
בֵּין אוֹר לְחֹשֶׁךְ, בֵּין יִשְׂרָאֵל לָעַמִּים, בֵּין יוֹם הַשְּׁבִיעִי לְשֵׁשֶׁת

OF BLESSINGS

יְמֵי הַמַּעֲשֶׂה. בָּרוּךְ אַתָּה ה' הַמַּבְדִּיל בֵּין קֹדֶשׁ לְחוֹל

Baruch atah, Adonai, Elohaynu melech ha'olam, hamavdil bayn kodesh lechol bayn or lechoshechbayn Yisrael la'amim bayn yom hashevi'i le-shayshet yemay hama'aseh. Baruch atah, Adonai, hamavdil bayn kodesh lechol.

Blessed are You, God, our Lord, Crowned Sovereign of the universe, who separates between the holy and the profane; between the light and dark; between Israel and the other nations; between the seventh day and the six days of the week. Blessed are You, God, who separates between the holy and the profane.

CHANUKAH BLESSINGS

After the shamash is lit (the helper candle) and before the actual Chanukah candles are lit, the following blessings are said.

FIRST BLESSING

בָּרוּךְ אַתָּה ה' אֱלֹקֵינוּ מֶלֶךְ הָעוֹלָם אֲשֶׁר קִדְּשָׁנוּ בְּמִצְוֹתָיו וְצִוָּנוּ לְהַדְלִיק נֵר חֲנֻכָּה

Ba-ruch A-tah Ado-nai E-lo-he-nu Me-lech ha-olam a-sher ki-de-sha-nu be-mitz-vo-tav ve-tzi-va-nu le-had-lik ner Cha-nu-kah.

Blessed are You, Lord our God, Crowned Sovereign of the universe, Who has sanctified us with His commandments, and commanded us to kindle the Chanukah light.

SECOND BLESSING

בָּרוּךְ אַתָּה ה' אֱלֹקֵינוּ מֶלֶךְ הָעוֹלָם שֶׁעָשָׂה נִסִּים לַאֲבוֹתֵינוּ בַּיָּמִים הָהֵם בִּזְמַן הַזֶּה

Ba-ruch A-tah Ado-nai E-lo-he-nu Me-lech Ha-olam she-a-sa ni-sim la-avo-te-nu ba-ya-mim ha-hem bi-zman ha-zeh.

Blessed are You, Lord our God, Crowned Sovereign of the universe, Who performed miracles for our forefathers in those days, at this time.

THIRD BLESSING

This blessing is recited only on the first night (or the first time lighting this Chanukah):

בָּרוּךְ אַתָּה ה' אֱלֹקֵינוּ מֶלֶךְ הָעוֹלָם שֶׁהֶחֱיָנוּ וְקִיְּמָנוּ וְהִגִּיעָנוּ לִזְמַן הַזֶּה

Ba-ruch A-tah Ado-nai E-lo-he-nu Me-lech Ha-olam she-heche-ya-nu ve-ki-yi-ma-nu ve-higi-a-nu liz-man ha-zeh.

Blessed are You, Lord our God, King of the universe, who has granted us life, sustained us, and enabled us to reach this occasion.

PASSOVER BLESSINGS

BLESSING FOR EATING MATZA AT THE SEDER

There are two blessings for eating matza at the Seder. The first is the same blessing we say when we eat bread—Hamotzi—and the second blessing is for the specific occasion of eating matza at the Seder.

בָּרוּךְ אַתָּה ה' אֱלֹקֵינוּ מֶלֶךְ הָעוֹלָם הַמּוֹצִיא לֶחֶם מן הָאָרֶץ

Baruch ata Adonai, Eloheinu Melech ha-olam, hamotzi lechem min ha'aretz.

Blessed are You, Lord our God, Crowned Sovereign of the universe, Who brings forth bread from the earth.

בָּרוּךְ אַתָּה ה' אֱלֹקֵינוּ מֶלֶךְ הָעוֹלָם, אֲשֶׁר קִדְּשָׁנוּ בְּמִצְוֹתָיו וְצִוָּנוּ עַל אֲכִילַת מַצָּה

Baruch atah A-do-nai, E-lo-hey-nu Melech ha-o-lam, asher kid-sha-nu b-mitz-vo-tav, v-tzi-van-nu al a-chilat matzah.

Blessed are You, Lord our God, Crowned Sovereign of the Universe, Who has sanctified us with His commandments and commanded us to eat matza.

BLESSING FOR EATING MAROR (BITTER HERBS)

Everyone takes some maror and dips it in the charoset. All then recite the following blessing, after which everyone should immediately eat their maror without leaning to the left (leaning is a sign of freedom).

בָּרוּךְ אַתָּה ה' אֱלֹקֵינוּ מֶלֶךְ הָעוֹלָם, אֲשֶׁר קִדְּשָׁנוּ בְּמִצְוֹתָיו
וְצִוָּנוּ עַל אֲכִילַת מָרוֹר

Ba'ruch Ah'tah Ah'doh'nai Eh'lo'hay'nu Melech ha'o'lam ah'sher kidishanu b'mitz'vo'tav v'tzee'vanu al ah'chee'laht ma'ror.

Blessed are You, Lord our God, Crowned Sovereign of the universe, Who has sanctified us with His commandments and commanded us to eat bitter herbs.

ABOUT THE AUTHORS

ELLYN HUTT inspires her students with classes that focus on practical Jewish spirituality. She has been bringing the wisdom of Torah and Judaism to life for over 30 years. She has a devoted following of students who have learned how Torah relates to their daily lives and guides them through challenges.

With a Master's degree in Economics, Ellyn describes her shift in focus from learning about "profits" to learning about "prophets." Her down-to-earth way of conveying the ancient wisdom of Torah in a vibrant way makes it relevant to a broad range of spiritual seekers from across the Jewish spectrum of practice and belief.

Ellyn also leads trips to Israel for women seeking a deeper connection to their Jewish identity. She has been married for 40 years and lives with her husband in Denver, Colorado. She has two married children and grandchildren living in New York City and Israel.

TEENA SLATKIN engages students of all ages through animated and thought-provoking storytelling focused on Jewish topics. She has embraced audiences for over 35 years with her vivacious style. She has also taught classes about women's issues for Jewish organizations, and has led inspiring spiritual missions to Israel for women from varied backgrounds.

Teena has a degree in Elementary and Special Education and is the author of the children's book, *LeRoy the Cowboy and His Magic Boot*, which won the Silver Medal for Children's Literature from the Colorado Independent Publishers' Association.

She is a passionate advocate promoting awareness about mental health within the Denver Jewish community. She has helped establish Bamidbar, the only Jewish, spiritual wilderness therapy program in North America, located in Colorado's Rocky Mountains.

Teena has been married for more than 40 years and lives with her husband in Denver, Colorado. She has four grown children and two grandchildren.